Failure's Not an Option

Dion Wingate

To [handwritten dedication] Thanks for your support [signature]

FORWARD

Sankofa is a word in the Twi language of Ghanians, whose literal translation means, "to go back and get it." The spirit of Sankofa is a metaphorical symbol generally depicted as a bird, with a neck extending backward to pick up an egg resting on it's back. It is the belief of the Akan people, that in Sankofa, one can't progress through life without remembering their past. And so it is with the story of Dion and this book, Failure's Not an Option.

As I began reading this book, I found myself experiencing the range of emotions Dion shared so freely. Those emotions ranged from awe, to sadness, to anger, to pain, and joy. There were moments I could identify with by virtue of my own life or by merely growing up in the same era as he. Whether or not you feel the same, to be sure, once you begin reading Failure's Not An Option, you will enjoy the series of events that lead to his "right now."

I found Dion's revised edition to be engaging and thought provoking. Indeed, Failure's Not An Option is a call to action. He challenges each of us not to lose sight of our past and to go back and get what's ours. Enjoy.

~Jonise M. Cromartie

DEDICATION

This book is dedicated to the following people:

Edithe Breedon Southerland
1905 – 1986

Annie Mae Southerland Blackwell
1922 – 1993

Lennel Williams, Sr.
Nickname "Hot Pot"
1925 - 1994

And a most heartfelt dedication goes out to my mother:

Betty Ann Blackwell Wingate
1948 – 1980

CONTENTS

ACKNOWLEDGMENTS

I'd like to thank Ebony Johnson for all of her editing work and Robert McIver for his exceptional graphics capabilities.

PROLOGUE

During these times of uncertainty, it's important to share moments of hope with one another. Just as I think I've reached a critical point in my life, a higher power, says to me, "I'm not finished with you yet." Like a rose out of concrete, I continue to grow. The moment I surrendered my troubles; my frustration; and guilt, my spirit felt anew. Throughout my life I always felt a sense of peace whenever situations seemed to be unbearable. I understand that sense of peace was a spiritual awakening. In fact, I was gaining spiritual strength to live a life of truth and accountability.

I am sharing my life experiences to encourage others to break the chains of fear and to live their purpose. I am living proof that the past does not determine your future. However, the past plays a role in the strength of your faith and integrity.

As you read this book, you will see how the higher power transitioned a child born to fail into a man who created his own success. Believe that from your vantage point, you have the power to change the perception of the negative circumstances that may surround you. Be transformative. Hold on to the notion: Failure's not an option.

"Well, son, I'll tell you:
Life for me ain't been no crystal stair.
It's had tacks in it,
And splinters,
And boards torn up,
And places with no carpet on the floor-
Bare.
But all the time
I'se been a climbin'on,
And reachin' landin's,
And turnin' corners,
And sometimes goin' in the dark
Where there ain't been no light.
So boy, don't you turn back.
Don't you set down on the steps
'Cause you finds it's kinder hard.
Don't you fall now-
For I'se still goin', honey,
I'se still climbin',
And life for me ain't been no crystal stair."
~ **Mother to Son, Langston Hughes**

1   BORN TO FAIL

There are some that believe that our story was written well before our birth. While we are given free will, our path has been predetermined. The obstacles we face along the way, strengthen our resolve.

On August 6, 1975, Linel Dion Wingate was born to a young mother, Betty Ann Blackwell. Prior to this birth, Betty married a hard working military man, Pernell Wingate. Together, they had three kids: Bridget, the oldest; Beverly, the middle child; and Pernell, Junior. Some say that she was too young to get married. However, in the late 1960s, being an African American woman from a small community, marrying a man in the military meant financial stability.

Betty was young, vibrant, and full of life. Not only did she miss her family, she became tired of the constant moving from city to city which was typical of a military lifestyle. The traditional housewife routine no longer worked for her. The stress of maintaining a household along with other issues she dealt with internally became unbearable. These feelings led Betty to experience a nervous breakdown. Eventually, the union came to an end and the two legally separated.

Now, Betty faced a new obstacle: taking care of herself and three children. After her divorce, she decided to move back home to be near her family in Sanford, North Carolina. By then, it was the 1970s and in a small town like Sanford, women were shunned for being divorced with small children or having a child out of wedlock.. Despite the judgment placed upon her, she did not let it stop her from bettering herself and enjoying life.

Betty was the type of woman that did not take kindly to being judged by others - that was grounds for verbal lashing. When it came to her children, she did not tolerate any mistreatment of them by anyone, young or old.

~

There was one event I recall my sister Beverly telling me about. At the age of thirteen, Beverly was bullied every day. One day, this bully decided to throw rocks and hit Beverly on the head. Word got back to our mother and let me say this, when she got a hold of that little girl, it wasn't anything nice. Let's just say, after that day, Beverly was never bullied again

~

Betty was a no-nonsense but loveable woman. she walked in the room all eyes were on her. She had caramel complexion skin, a coke bottle body shape, and long beautiful legs. She had the most beautiful white teeth ever seen and the confidence to match her beauty. As a result, she made a lot of women jealous and didn't have many women friends.

Despite everything, Betty was determined to beat all the odds stacked against her. She did not want to be another woman with children, being supported by the government like the two generations before her.

As such, Betty decided to become a registered nurse. Even though the nursing school Betty attended was an hour away, Betty's journey displayed her determination to succeed. Failure was not an option for Betty. When she did not have access to transportation, Betty would hitchhike to make it to school. She remained steadfast , not giving up and following her spiritual compass.. Eventually, with hard work and sacrifice Betty achieved her goal of becoming a registered nurse.

While maintaining a career, and being a full-time mother, she met an attractive man named Linel Williams. Linel had a background in the military like her ex-husband Pernell. Unlike Pernell, he was attending college to become a teacher. The relationship between Betty and Linel escalated quickly and was short-lived. What they did not know was another life lived inside of Betty.

Betty was faced with a difficult choice - to have an abortion or choose to raise a child without the assistance of a father. Being that Betty never seemed to play victim of circumstance, she made the decision to keep her child.. Betty had three children and was already divorced, with another one on the way. That was a "don't do" in her small community. However, Betty ignored the negative talk about her being pregnant with her fourth child. To her, they may have said things behind her back, but no one was bold enough to say them to her face. Remember, she was a no-nonsense woman.

Throughout the pregnancy she had the support of her three children but not many family members or Linel. A strong bond was built between Betty and her three children during that time. The children felt they had Betty to themselves for once, especially the two girls Bridget and Beverly. Until the fourth child was born.

~

From the beginning Bridget and Beverly were extremely protective of me, the fourth child. As I got older, at two or three years of age, my brother Pernell became my enemy because he had always been the baby. At a young age, I knew how to upset my big brother. Pernell had a set of Star Trek cards that he cherished and I would take them when he wasn't looking and would hide them.

One day I thought he had left the room so I took one of his cards and ran. He stuck out his foot and tripped, causing me to strike my head on the bedpost and split my eye open. Pernell gained two more enemies that day: Bridget and Beverly, the two oldest. Oddly enough, he also gained a fan because, when I returned from the hospital, he gave me his Star Trek cards. Life with my siblings was all I knew. It was the only time in my life my spirit felt real love.

Then one day, without warning, my life would change forever. I can't erase the memory of my mother: tears running down her face as she drove off. The memory is so vivid. Confrontation ensued between my mother and great-grandmother, Edith Sutherland. They were struggling over my luggage. I was supposed to get on a plane with my mother that day. My great-grandmother would not let her take me. They both were tugging at the suitcase, my clothes strewn all over the lawn; "You can't just take my baby!"Those were the last words I heard my mother scream before jumping in her car and driving away.

Later, I learned that my mother had died in a plane crash on her way to Vineland, New Jersey. I was only four years old..

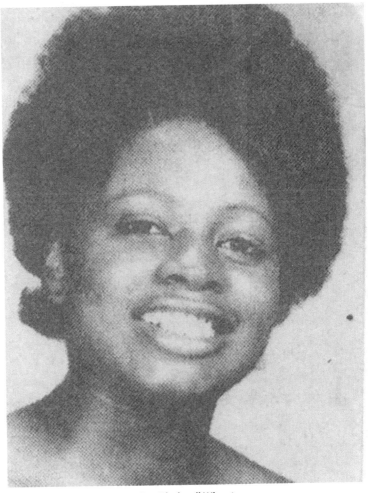

Betty Ann Blackwell Wingate

1948 - 1980

A few days after my mother was laid to rest, my siblings, Bridget, Beverly, and Pernell moved to live with their father. They moved 300 miles away to Lanham, Maryland. At a young age, I remember feeling alone and scared. The security I'd once known could no longer protect me. The cherished baby of a loving family was now an orphaned child that no one wanted.

Failure is not an option; it was instilled in my psyche as a child. Evidenced by my grandmother, Annie Mae Blackwell's decision to take me in. Once I realized that the only family I had known was not coming back, I soon accepted Annie Mae as being my only family. As I adjusted to my new family, I no longer addressed Annie Mae as grandma. Instead, I began addressing her as "Mama."

Mama was old school. She loved the outdoors and fishing was one of her hobbies. I can remember her taking me on fishing trips and she would curse me out for talking so much and say I was scaring the fish. My attachment to her grew because at the time, she was all I had. In my mind, I was afraid that I would lose her like I did my siblings; my mother. The funny thing is, I was so attached to Mama that until the age of 10, I slept at the foot of her bed until she determined I was too old. I would even hide in her car when I knew she was going somewhere without me. Mama knew how to make me feel special. One of my fondest memories was when she cooked, she would make me a personal pan of biscuits with molasses; I loved that.

As I grew older, Mama felt I needed to interact with other kids. One summer she sent me to 4-H camp for two weeks. The 4-H camp was one of my best childhood experiences. I was surrounded by kids of different nationalities and cultures; I felt free.

One of the counselors took special interest in me. I can't recall his name, but he would introduce me to the kids in different groups and would encourage me to participate in activities that would intimidate me, such as swimming. I remember the last day being difficult for me. Yet again I had to reconcile the feeling of being taken from an environment where I felt I belonged. As I was boarding the bus, the counselor I'd formed a bond with gave me his telephone number. It was as if he knew and understood my sadness; an unspoken acknowledgement that said to me, "hey, failure is not an option."

I cried the entire bus ride home. Once I arrived home, I stayed in the house for a week. 4-H camp changed my outlook on the world and the experience made me realize that there were possibilities outside of Mama's house.

Shortly after I got over the trauma of leaving the 4-H camp I became sociable with the kids in my community, known as the old projects. The kids in the old projects would knock on my door every day after school, only to get cursed out by Mama. Clearly, she was not used to the disturbance.

Eventually the kids would knock on the door and run before she would answer. We developed a knock and run code that signified a message for me to play outside Every Saturday morning my little crew would meet at the same spot to plan our adventure. All of us had vivid imaginations, like the time we built a raft made out of sticks, a few logs and string. We worked on the raft for at least two weeks. Our plan was to sail far away from our homes, destination unknown.

The day arrived. The raft was complete and after school, the plan was to leave and sail away. We placed the raft in the shallow water. Like fools, we all jumped on and it sank! At this point, everyone was looking at each other in disbelief coupled with the fear of what our parents would say after seeing our muddy and smelly school clothes.

On the way home, everyone began crying and blaming each other. I decided to walk home as slowly as I possibly could. Mama was waiting for me at the door. One of the parents must have called her to discuss our foolishness because before I could make it all the way in the house, I was greeted with a swinging switch. You couldn't tell her she didn't pick that switch with tender, loving care.

Mama did her best to provide for and raise a respectful, young boy. I was around the age of 11 when I heard her having a heated conversation with a man in the living room of our house. I recall being curious to see who she was talking to. As I peered in the room, our eyes met, "go back to your room!", she exclaimed. Eventually Mama called me into the living room to meet, who I'd learn was my father. He was well dressed, groomed, and spoke with what was considered to be proper English. The man stared at me and started to ask me questions about myself. We made small talk as I told him the type of toys I liked and what I did in school. Mama addressed the man as Linel. Though I was confused about this man, with whom I shared the same name, I immediately felt a connection. In a frustrated tone, mama said, 'this boy needs some shoes.' Linel then answered, 'ok, what size shoe does he wear?' She could not answer because most of the shoes I owned were second hand. Mama gave Linel one of my so called good shoes to use as a tool to get my correct shoe size.

When Linel left the house, I stood in the doorway until I couldn't see his car anymore. I felt excitement after meeting Linel. I couldn't wait until he returned with my new shoes. I remember telling everyone in the neighborhood my dad's name and how he was dressed and how he was getting me a pair of new shoes.

A week passed and there were no new shoes or Linel. Mama was upset and continuously repeated to me 'I should have never let him meet you because I knew all Linel would do is disappoint you'. I wished that Linel would prove her wrong. Every day,I stood in the doorway looking at every car that passed by in hopes that Linel would pull up.

A month had passed since Linel was supposed to return to our house with my new shoes. I'd grown accustomed to people not returning in my life. My mother, my siblings, and now Linel. Having low expectations of others shielded me in many ways from further disappointment. I began growing in my mantra, "Failure is not an option."

Eventually Linel resurfaced 6 months later and became more active in my life. Linel became more consistent with his visits and Mama began to trust him a little more. I remember one Friday after school, I returned home and was told by Mama, 'pack your bag, you're going to spend the night with Linel.' I felt scared

17

and excited at the same time because the only other time I stayed away from home was during the 4-H camp.

Linel came to pick me up that evening. The anticipation of waiting felt like days instead of hours. While walking outside, I noticed the extremely nice car - the type of car that I had seen on TV. It was a gold toned, fancy body style with the lion-type emblem. I noticed the tan leather seats. At that moment, I no longer felt like a poor project kid. I felt more like a privileged kid.

When we pulled off, I hoped some of my friends saw me in such a fancy car. As we got closer to our destination Linel informed me that I would be meeting my brother and sister. At that moment, I was a little confused because the only siblings I knew about had moved to Maryland with their father. Linel and I pulled up to our destination. My feelings of nervousness intensified. This was my first time staying overnight with him and I had no clue who the brother and sister he mentioned were. When we walked through the door, I was greeted by an older woman that acknowledged herself as my grandmother. From the living room, I could see two kids playing who were definitely younger than me. Linel walked me into the room where the little kids were.

Linel introduced us by telling me, 'your brother's name is Lee and your sister's name is Nefertiti.' After getting over the initial shock, we began interacting and soon it felt as if we belonged together. The connection I felt with them mirrored the connection I felt with my siblings that had been taken away from me as a young four year old child.

Over the course of that weekend, Linel went from being addressed as 'Sir' to 'dad.' When I returned back home, things would not be the same. Whenever Mama would ask me to do something I didn't want to do, I'd tell her I wanted to live with my dad. I ignored the sacrifice she'd made in her life to raise her daughter's child.

I became rebellious in hopes that I would be sent to live with my dad. Mama started to regret that she introduced me to him because of the change in my attitude. Just as before, Linel's consistency came to a halt and I was left with the feelings of emptiness. This time, I started taking out my anger on the one constant force in my life, Mama. I started staying out late, hanging out with the older guys in the neighborhood and talking back.

One day I had gotten in trouble in school. The principal called me to his office, sat back in his chair and told me I wouldn't live to see 16. The principal did little to encourage me. Instead, he destroyed my innocence and made me feel hopeless. Words have power. The words of the principal on that day, negatively impacted my life.

Once I possessed that spirit of hopelessness, I began to attract the kind of people who also felt hopeless. The older guys that I would hang out with in the neighborhood introduced me to alcohol as a joke. One of the guys thought it would be funny to see a 12year-old drunk, I guess, so he gave me a beer and I drank it. That was one of the worst choices I could've made in my life. I couldn't stand the taste but loved the feeling it gave me. For a time, the idea of failure not being an option, came to a screeching halt.

2   LOSER IN THE MAKING

I was almost a teenager and growing more rebellious by the day when I started to explore the street life. I was impressed by the respect my cousin Raymond and his friends received in the neighborhood. Raymond lost his mother but in a different way than I did. His mother wanted no part of him when he was born and his father, which is my uncle Charles, was a free-spirited playboy who moved to Detroit, Michigan. It was my great-grandmother Edith who took him in the same way Mama took me in. In a way, we both were adopted by our grandparents. Raymond was 10 years older than me and eventually became my role model.

Although Raymond was the neighborhood drug dealer, he was the coolest person on the planet to me. I remember bragging to my friends about how cool the Adidas sweat suits and matching shoes looked on Raymond and his crew before they hit the block. The meeting spot for Raymond and his friends was the back room of my great grandmother's house.

When I was at my great grandmother's house, I could always make a couple of dollars off Raymond and his friends. They would have me starch and iron their clothes or pay me to let them know when someone was at the door while they were conducting business. One day when Raymond and his friends were out, I was snooping around his room and I found supply bags, scissors and rolling papers-drug paraphernalia.

I did not anticipate Raymond and his friends returning to the room so soon. I had no time to leave so I hid in the closet. It felt like I was in the closet forever. I peeked out only to see them smoking, bagging and weighing marijuana. I was no stranger to seeing marijuana, but I had never seen such a large quantity. While I was watching through a crack in the closet door, I saw where Raymond would stash his product. Within a little less than an hour hiding in the closet I gained a lesson in dealing.

What I learned that day changed my life. In school I became known as the candyman. I would buy five cent candy from the corner store which was Petty Groceries and sell it in school for twenty-five cents. My customers were mostly white kids who weren't allowed to have candy at home. One day one of those kids asked me if I could get him some marijuana. I asked the kid how much he wanted. He told me ten dollars' worth.

Now at that time, ten dollars was a lot of money to me. It took me almost two weeks to make ten dollars from selling candy. I had no clue what ten dollars' worth of marijuana looked like, but I remember where Raymond stashed it and the envelopes he and his friends would use for packaging. After school that day, I went down to my great grandmother's house and as usual Raymond and his friends were in the room conducting business.

I waited patiently until they left the room and snuck in and found his stash that hadn't changed from a couple of weeks ago. I grabbed one of the envelopes and stuffed it to the top with marijuana and carefully made sure everything was in place. I entered the room and fled, in fear of Raymond and his friends returning.

When I arrived at school the next day, I found the white kid that inquired about marijuana and showed him what I had. The white kid seemed to be impressed with the package. After a week or so went by, the white and his friends began inquiring for more.

Now I was making more money in a couple of days than I ever did off candy. I was also stealing from Raymond's stash and that became noticeable too. Raymond was beginning to ask questions like 'has anyone been in my room?' I decided it was best to slow down, taking from Raymond.

A couple of months after I found my new business, Raymond got incarcerated. With Raymond being incarcerated, I had no access to the product but I had a good reputation amongst the kids along with my clientele. One of my friends who was the same age as me but way more advanced in the drug game heard about my little business and decided to let me venture into his. At the time, I did not know there was a difference between selling drugs on the street versus in the school but I would learn fast. My strategy in school did not work on the streets so I had to adjust. Now as a kid with no money, I was starting to understand the power of money. I admit, I enjoyed the attention of being labeled a drug dealer. The lifestyle I was involved in seemed natural because the majority of my friends had transitioned into drug dealers.

We would come to school with gold rings on every finger and gold chains around our necks. The teachers and the staff knew that our parents couldn't afford the material items we obtained. The girls in school started to notice me. One white girl named Amy started sending me notes in class telling me how funny and cute I was.

One day Amy and I got caught sending notes back and forth in class and we were sent to after school detention. The day Amy and I had to stay after school would change both of our lives forever. Amy at the

24

time, had a redneck boyfriend named Brent who didn't care too much for blacks. Somehow Amy, during our conversation became sexual. With hormones racing, Amy and I found a spot in the woods behind the school to kill our curiosity.

I was completely inexperienced at sex and had no knowledge of condoms so we had unprotected sex. Amy's boyfriend Brent found out somehow that Amy and I had intercourse and was furious. I started hearing rumors of Brent telling people that he was going to kill me. I contacted one of the white kids that I sold marijuana to and inquired about a gun because he would always talk about hunting and going to the shooting range with his dad.

The kid told me he would get me a gun in exchange for some drugs so of course that was a deal for me. The kid met with me the next day after school with a long nose 22 and holster. This was my first time holding a gun and it gave me a feeling of power. The kid and I made the transaction and I took the gun and headed back to class.

Between the time I got to class and the transaction, word around school got out that I had a gun and I was going to kill Brent. During the break, in between classes some of my friends asked me to see the gun I purchased. I hadn't told anyone I had a gun but everyone seemed to know, which made me nervous.

I was sitting in the last class of the day when I heard my name called over the intercom to report to my aunt's classroom. I found that kind of odd, that I had to report to my aunt's classroom instead of the principal's office. My aunt was my mother's older sister. Cherville had been teaching at the school for over 20 years and she had a relationship with the staff.

I hesitated before entering my aunt's classroom because I knew this couldn't be good. As I walked into the room, I noticed the school principal was sitting in the class also. My heart dropped as I went to have a seat and to find out what was the urgency of the meeting.

The principal started the conversation with a little small talk then he got to the real reason why I was called to the classroom. The principal stated that he heard rumors that I had a gun on campus but he honestly didn't believe it. By the look on his face though, I knew that was a lie. When the principal asked me if I had a gun I nervously said no and asked him why would I have one?

My aunt then looked relieved but the principal didn't seem to be satisfied with my answer so he told me that I need to do one more thing to make him feel secure. I asked him what that was, and he told me he

26

needed me to take off my coat. I hesitated, looked at my aunt, her eyes now filled with disappointment, as I looked at the principal. He had the look of fear in his eyes. I jumped up and ran out of the classroom into the woods behind the school.

I stashed the gun which turned out to be a great idea because by the time I made it out of the woods, the police were waiting for me. The police patted me down and found no gun so they had to let me go. One of the officers asked, 'if you had no gun why did you run?' to which I replied, 'because I had rolling papers in my pocket and that would've caused me to be expelled if they were found.' Despite the gun not being found, I still managed to get suspended from the Lee County school system indefinitely. I was now 12 going on 13 and kicked out of school.

To add to the problem, I received a phone call from Amy, the white girl that was in my class informing me she was pregnant and I was the father. The phone conversation with Amy was one of the most terrifying conversations I had experienced. The emotions I felt at that point in time were immense fear. My response to Amy was, 'You can't be pregnant by me; we only had sex one time.' I called Amy every name in the book and told her never to call me again because I knew if Mama found out, that would be my one-way ticket out of her house.

Now dealing with the stress of the streets, getting kicked out of school, and a white girl possibly being pregnant by me, I found two outlets - one was music with my cousin Ralph Sutherland who became like a big brother to me once Raymond got incarcerated. Ralph was also respected in the neighborhood but not for dealing drugs but for being tough and a great MC. Ralph was the one person I could tell anything in the world to and he wouldn't be judgmental.

My other outlet became alcohol which at the time gave me a total escape from my dysfunctional reality. Once I was kicked out of school, I was living a double life. I would make music and listen to Ralph who was trying to get me back on track and keep me out of trouble. At night, I was selling drugs and getting drunk with my friends.

At the age of 12, I started drinking alcohol daily. I had a crew of kids my age that loved to drink. There was also one guy that hung around us who was old enough to purchase alcohol. Back then, it was cool to drink 40 ounces of Old English and we would drink at least two throughout the day. While my other drinking partners would be in school during the week, I would be hanging out with the guy that could buy beer named Derek, getting drunk.

Derek had the ID and I had the money to purchase the alcohol. Soon, I was drinking more alcohol than

28

hustling. The downside to that was that I was working on consignment and people expected their money from the drugs they fronted me. When I was under the influence of alcohol, any amount of danger I put my family and myself in no longer mattered. I began not coming home some nights and being totally disrespectful to Mama.

I recall one morning I was being mouthy to Mama and she called the sheriff who was a friend of hers to the house. Surprisingly, the sheriff had already heard about me and my mischief in the streets. The sheriff looked me in my eyes as I was being mannish and disrespectful to him and told me, 'you are headed down the same road as your cousin Raymond'. The sheriff looked at my grandmother in a disappointing way and said, 'the only other suggestion I have for you is to send him to reform school.'

Things in the house got so out of control until she had no other option but to kick me out. Once Mama told me and other family members that I had to leave her house, I thought I would just go to my dad's house and live happily ever after like I'd always wanted. That did not happen.

Linel gave me every excuse for why I could not live with him. While on the phone with my dad, I listened as he rejected me. I told him I understood, all while crying like a baby. I then realized everything Mama ever told me was true. However, I would never admit she was right about Linel.

Without many living options in Sanford, North Carolina my older sister Beverly who was a young single mother herself and lived in Washington DC, decided to take on the responsibility of her little brother. The one she barely knew who was a drug dealing, alcoholic, rebellious adolescent.

3   LEAVING MY PROBLEMS AND BAD HABITS BEHIND

The family came together to purchase me a one way ticket out of Sanford NC. As I packed my bags with a smirk on my face while looking back at Mama, she just smiled and told me something that I would always remember. She looked at me with a straight face and said, "You will see the difference when my head turns cold." I acted as though the words she said didn't faze me but the truth was, those words she said sent chills up my spine.

I loaded a trash bag and some raggedy luggage into the trunk of Mama's car. The ride to the bus station was silent and the closer we got to the bus station, the more I started second-guessing my decision to leave because honestly, Mama practically raised me. As I boarded the bus I felt sad because I didn't know what to expect when I got to DC. For the first hour of my bus ride, I cried because I started feeling guilty about all the hell I had put Mama through. I cried myself to sleep and when I awoke I heard the bus driver announce you have now arrived in Washington DC.

As I got off the bus I felt anxious and nervous at the same time. When I saw my brother Pernell and sister Beverly and their looks of excitement, the nervousness I felt went away. I believed I was ready to start my new life. Even though we were all separated over the years, the connection I felt was as if I was finally home. I felt like I returned to my essence and the missing links of my life, my siblings. I remember my three older siblings holding a meeting of how they all would come together to fix the mess their little brother had caused for himself. It was an amazing effort, being that Bridget, the oldest of Betty's four children, now had three kids of her own. She had a boy Dante, and his younger brother Darrell. Beverly, who also was a single mom, had a daughter named Brittany. Pernell, had just started his life in a career on the Washington police force and had a daughter named Gabrielle.

To be honest, now looking back, my three siblings were trying to fix something that could not be fixed, me. The three decided that it would be best that I move in with Beverly. At the beginning, Beverly and I had a great relationship. She gave the nurturing of a mother that I had missed throughout my life.

Beverly had an apartment in uptown Northwest Washington DC where I adapted to the neighborhood fast. I can remember my first day exploring the neighborhood by myself. I was just a small-town boy fresh out of Sanford, North Carolina with what they called a high-top fade which was cool in Sanford but which I soon found out was outdated in DC. While on my exploration of the neighborhood, a group of guys

32

on the corner pointed out my outdated hairstyle. I could hear them making jokes and laughing so I began walking faster. After feeling humiliated by the hairstyle which I thought was so cool, I made it back to my new home.

A couple of days after that incident my brother Pernell came to pick me up to hang out. The first thing Pernell said when I entered the car was, "little brother you look like a Bama with your hair like that so I'm going to take you to the barbershop." I objected because in my mind, my high-top fade was cool and the people in DC just didn't know what was happening in the world. Pernell finally used his authority as a big brother and said, "Look, the hightop fade must go." While I was sitting in the barber chair, I was upset to see big chunks of my hair being cut. After the haircut, to cheer me up, Pernell took me out to eat. I still was upset with Pernell for making me cut my high-top fade until I started to notice the young ladies in the restaurant showing me attention.

When I pointed out to Pernell how the young ladies in the restaurant were staring at me, he just laughed and said, "This is just the beginning little brother." It felt good to have a big brother to help me transition into my New World. I had left Sanford, North Carolina at the beginning of summer and now I was officially a teenager, 13 years old in a new city.

The summer was coming to an end and Beverly and I started having conversations about me enrolling in school. I knew that enrolling me in school would be a challenge because of me being expelled from the Lee County school system indefinitely. Gripp inside, I was growing nervous the more Beverly was considering my history and mischief in the Lee County school system. I had the fear that Beverly would find out that her little brother wasn't as innocent as he portrayed himself to be. In the midst of Beverly conversing back and forth with the school system another problem arose.

The problem that I thought went away had now resurfaced. The white girl Amy that had claimed to be pregnant by me had found a way to get in contact with my family. Amy's parents insisted that she give the child up for adoption but with her claiming that I was the child's father, she could not do anything without my consent. Now everyone in the family knew that I had a child and to make matters worse, with a white girl. Reality was now starting to set in. I realize that all the problems that I thought were gone, never went away. I was just a child myself, how could I be a father?

Eventually, the agency that Amy was going through for adoption informed me that the baby in question was a girl. The people at the agency informed me that if I signed over my rights as a parent, that the baby girl would be placed into a nice home with caring parents.

This was one of the first times I felt completely powerless. No longer did I feel that Amy was trying to frame me with a child. I felt the apparent connection with this baby girl in question that I can't explain, being I never held the little girl. The agency and I finally came to an agreement that if I signed the papers, they would leave the file open so the child could find me if she had an interest in locating her biological parent.

Until this present day, I still do not understand how a document could be valid with the signature of a minor. Finally, the paperwork for the adoption was finalized and the agency must have heard the concern in my voice and decided to send me a picture of the baby girl who was named Jamie by her adopted parents. With that situation out of the way, Beverly managed to get me enrolled into school.

Paul Middle School was the only school that would give me an opportunity. My first couple of months at school were productive. Around the fourth month in school the troubled kids started to gravitate towards me. When I look back, I realize that there is truth in "you receive the energy that you put out." History started to repeat itself. Here, I was considered the class clown, disruptive and disrespectful.

I met this one kid named Terry who had the same attitude I had about school. Terry was what the students considered a cool kid and the teachers

35

considered to be a loser. Terry was no stranger to the streets and slowly began to show me the ropes. Terry was into stealing cars and petty drug dealing. I soon began not showing up for school and hanging out with Terry. Hanging out with Terry was one of the most adventurous times in my life because I got to learn the DC street life.

At one point in time I could remember Terry had three stolen cars stashed behind his apartment building. He had two 280Zs and one hooptie. At that time, I did not realize the risk I was taking hanging out with Terry but I can say, it was fun. Some days when we would skip school, he would let me follow him to other middle schools in one of the stolen cars to pick up girls. It was surprising how impressed the girls our age were over the cars we were driving. Terry and I began to use the cars as an advantage to get the girls to skip school and hang out with us.

Now at this time, Beverly was working two jobs to take care of her daughter Brittany and me. With Beverly being away from home so much, it gave Terry and I a place to bring the girls we would meet. Beverly only had two rules: One was for me to go to school every day and two, to pick my niece Brittany up from daycare daily. But as I started slipping back into old habits, I began picking up Brittany late which in turn forced

Beverly to pay a fee. I was barely going to school and who I really was began to resurface.

One day Terry and I were riding around and I met a young lady that would again change the course of my life. The young lady I met was named Tina. She was really cute, what we would call a fly girl back then. Tina was different. I actually had an interest in her because she also seemed to be street-smart. I was visiting Tina one day and her uncle came by her house. I could tell what line of business he was in by the way he dressed. I guess he could tell that I was no stranger to the street by my disposition.

Tina introduced me to her uncle and he introduced himself as Ali. He told me he just moved from Cali. Soon, her uncle and I began talking street talk. Ali seemed to take an interest in me the same way the older guys in Sanford, North Carolina did. Before I left Tina's house that day, her uncle and I exchanged phone and beeper numbers.

Shortly after the first meeting, Ali began fronting me packages of cocaine to sell. Now I was full-fledged back to my old ways but with an added street skill. Business with Ali soon began to overshadow my relationship with his niece. Terry and I started hanging out less because my interests changed. I was lucky if I went to school once a week now because my main objective was to make money. I didn't have to go far

37

from home to set up shop because less than a block from where I was staying, was a drug strip.

The same guys that made fun of my flat top haircut when I first moved to the neighborhood were now my friends. It was only a matter of time before Beverly would find out what I was involved in, so I would never let her see me on the block. I would duck and hide if she would walk in that direction to get home. I was back to living a double life. I acted like I had been in school all day and would try to pick up my niece on time throughout the week while in between those times I would be peddling drugs for Ali.

One day I came home and stashed drugs in my shoe. Beverly had to move my shoes for some reason. In the process of Beverly moving my shoes she noticed a Ziploc sandwich bag with a lot of little baggies that contained a white substance.

Beverly confronted me about the Ziploc with the baggies. It was clear, she had no clue what the substance was. I could see more disappointment in her eyes than I did anger. I told her I was holding the package for a friend. From the look on her face I could tell she wanted to believe that was the truth but I knew she didn't buy it. I was exposed as the lying, mischief teenager family and friends warned her about. I admit that it hurt me really bad to know that someone who sacrificed and believed in me was so disappointed in me, but at that time in my life I had somehow lost hope in myself. From that day, onward, the relationship between Beverly and myself went downhill.

Beverly no longer questioned me about going to school and she found someone else to pick up my niece from daycare. She also gave me a deadline to move out of the house because she felt as though my lifestyle was putting her and my niece in danger. On top of that, she was about to get married and move out of the city to Maryland with no plans of me coming along.

Time got closer to Beverly moving on with her life. I started feeling scared on the inside but on the outside looking unfazed. I was now faced with the fear of living on my own at 16 in a city where my only family were my associates in the streets. To add to the fear, I hadn't heard from Ali in weeks.

Ali would always come and pick up his money from me at least twice a week. The weeks turned into months and I spent Ali's money as well as mine. The day came when Beverly got married and moved out of the apartment but she informed me that I could stay in the apartment as long as I paid rent. That sounded good but now my connection was nowhere to be found and I had no money. I didn't know the first thing about paying bills.

When Beverly moved out of the apartment, she took everything with her, down to the shower curtains. I remember my first night staying alone in the empty apartment. I slept on the floor using my coat as a cushion and I cried myself to sleep that night. That was also the night I built a relationship with my deceased mother.

While I was lying there on the floor scared and crying in a fetal position, I felt the energy of my mother rocking me to sleep as if I were a baby. The next two nights were a little easier, being that I had someone to talk to and hold me.

On the outside, I appeared to be a tough guy but on the inside I was just a lost 16-year-old kid. I did not leave the apartment for about the first three days. I guess I was in shock. I survived off eating nacho chips and sour cream that was left behind when Beverly moved out of the apartment. From my childhood, I had learned how to not show my true emotions.

When Beverly or her new husband would come and check the mail, I would disguise my pain and act as though I was having the time of my life. I had learned at a young age that you never give anyone the pleasure of knowing your pain.

One day I was trying to get into the building where I was living and it just so happened Beverly's friend

Mickey was entering the building and let me in. Mickey started asking questions about how Beverly was doing and she had no clue that Beverly had moved. Mickey then realized that I was in the apartment by myself with no food or bed to sleep on. She became my lifesaver but didn't realize it. Mickey made her son give me a mattress off his bed to take upstairs to the apartment and a black-and-white TV. Mickey informed me that I could come to her house at 5:00 every evening to eat dinner. Now when I look back, I realize that people are placed in our lives for a reason. Mickey had to be a selfless woman to invite a child she barely knew into her home when she was already a mother of three children, her son being the same age as me. Eventually I started to feel whole again.

I found a new drug connection that fronted me packages and I was back on the block again. Now the apartment that I once felt lonely in was the hang out for me and my friends. To them, I was "the man" because I had my own place, or so they thought. I started recognizing the power I had over girls because they would sneak out of their homes to spend the night with me on the floor with one mattress. Some of the girls would bring food from home and different care products I needed. It almost felt as though the young ladies wanted to take care of me. It became no challenge for me to seduce and have my way with girls my age anymore. I knew exactly what to tell them to get what I wanted.

4   ATTRACTING THE ENERGY I PUT OUT

The feelings of loneliness were being filled with multiple girls. To feel validated, I needed to talk to or be intimate with different girls. Throughout my time of being promiscuous I met a young lady named Diana.

Diana was different than the typical young girls I was dealing with at that time in my life. She had a daughter and was much more mature and responsible than I was. Diana and I soon began to hang out every day. At the time, she was in school and working. I wasn't used to girls my age having jobs.

I was honest with Diana about my fears and unstable living conditions. I found someone that I could express my true feelings but unfortunately I still could not remain faithful.

Less than a month of dating Diana, I ran into a big problem. Without paying rent or utilities, I was no longer able to live in my apartment. I started to feel as though I was cursed. I finally met a young lady whom I could share everything with and would have to reveal that I was homeless.

Now with nowhere to go, my older sister Bridget offered a temporary solution. She had four little kids, three boys and one girl that she was raising in a two-bedroom apartment. Even though by now my siblings realized they had bit off more than they could chew, they still came together to give their little brother a new start in life.

The option that they came up with was job corps, which at the time sounded so bad. But I didn't have many other options. I discussed this with Diana, who had by then become my exclusive girlfriend. We discussed my plans of getting my life on track by going to job corps. In the midst of the discussion Diana got quiet and started crying and went on to tell me that she was pregnant.

My heart immediately dropped and I honestly started to believe that every time something seemed to go right in my life something bad had to occur. I was still carrying the guilt of how I treated Amy, the white girl who became pregnant when I was 13. I had a different, more mature response with Diana because I refused to have another adoption story, like Jamie, my first child. I had no clue what I was going to do to raise a child. However, I began to believe going to the job corps to learn a skill was not a bad decision; particularly for the future of my child. When my family found out that I was going to be a father they had mixed feelings. All I thought was,, "I will go to the job corps and prove them wrong."

44

Being that Diana was pregnant, I chose the location that was an hour outside of Washington DC in Laurel, Maryland. The first two weeks in the job corps I did well and soon met friends from DC who had the same street mentality as me.

About the third week in job corps, old habits started to resurface. My new found friends and I learned how to sneak in alcohol on campus. Not even a full month in the job corps, my friends and I were being promiscuous with the women and selling a little marijuana on campus.

One day, I will never forget. While I was in class I got a call to the office. Once I got to the office I saw my sister looking sad and the head of the facility asked me to have a seat. My sister was completely silent as the head of the facility told me I could have a two week leave. The first thing that came to my mind was that either the sneaking alcohol on campus or selling had caught up with me. That was not the case. When I got to my sister's car I got in and she was still silent, but she handed me a pack of cigarettes. I was feeling nervous and confused.

She finally spoke and told me Annie Mae, the grandmother I called Mama had passed away. My emotions were going crazy because this was the first time I lost someone that I was truly emotionally attached to. I cried for a short period of time and then

45

thought about the words that she had told me: "You will see the difference when my head turns cold."

I soon found out, truer words had never been spoken. The emotional wall I built automatically reappeared. At the funeral, I realized how much I really loved and missed Mama. I remember when I said my final goodbyes and how cold I felt when I kissed her forehead while she lay in the casket. When I returned to the job corps, a part of my soul got buried with Mama.

The truth is, a person can change who they attract by certain clothes they wear but have no control over who they attract by the energy they give. I met a guy who was just like me – a street kid who lost his mother at a young age and he also lived with his sister. My new found friend's name was Nate. Nate lived in Washington DC not far from the neighborhood I had recently lived in.

Eventually Nate and I decided that job corps wasn't for us and we both hated following rules so we came up with the plan to get kicked out of job corps. We decided to walk through the girl's dormitory and cuss out the staff. The plan to get kicked out worked but neither of us had a place to live when we got back to DC because his sister was finished with his behavior as was mine. To make money we bagged up fake drugs

46

and sold them to get real drugs wholesale in order to make a profit.

Nate and I finally started making a little money and started giving people drugs in exchange for a place to stay or car to drive. That year, on the fourth of July weekend I stayed over at my older sister Bridget's house to hang out with my family. I got a call from Nate. He asked me where I was. I told him. But this day, I didn't have a good feeling and I did not follow my intuition.

Nate called to tell me he needed me to go to a cookout with him because the girl that he had met had a friend for me. I agreed to go and Nate finally showed up. This time I noticed something about the car Nate was driving. It had a tile over the ignition. I was no stranger to stolen cars because that was my friend Terry's forte but being that it was a nice car, I paid no attention.

I just wanted to drive it so I could feel big. Nate finally agreed to let me drive. I was now behind the wheel of this nice car at such a young age and it made me feel empowered. Not ten minutes into the ride, I notice a cop car behind us and Nate begins to look nervous as he tells me to speed up. I accelerated and the cop seemed to accelerate. When I made a turn, it seemed like the cop car made a turn.

Finally, the cop hit the lights and out of nowhere another police car blocks us in without an exit. The car that made me feel so empowered now made me feel extremely vulnerable. As the police put me in the back of their car I was informed that the car was, indeed, stolen. Due to it being a holiday weekend and me being a juvenile I was placed in the maximum-security 23-hour lockdown. I had plenty of time to think. Strangely, the first thought that I had was how Diana, who was carrying my child would be disappointed in me. Afterall, she was under the impression that I was still in the job corps.

I was in jail almost two weeks before I received a visit. The person that I had put the most under stress during that year, my sister Beverly. It was Beverly that came to visit me. When I got to the visiting room, there was a glass that separated us. Beverly started crying immediately after seeing me, her little brother in shackles.

The first thing Beverly said to me was she was that she was trying to prevent me from being incarcerated. I responded by telling her that I didn't feel bad. In my mind, a person could only change if they want to change and I had no intentions of changing myself.

That was my way of taking accountability for my actions. I stayed locked up for about two weeks after that visit and got released on pretrial to Beverly. By this time, Beverly had moved to upper Marlboro, Maryland.

Strangely enough, that was where I was locked up. I guess once again, Beverly was trying to save someone who did not want to be saved. History soon would repeat itself even though I was confined to the neighborhood. My energy still attracted the same people.

Being on house arrest only made my old habits resurface. I started drinking alcohol more often and was now starting to alter my attitude. My love for women didn't change. I started dating multiple girls in the neighborhood.

I started dating a young lady named Tanya. She had light skin with green eyes and a nice body. She only lived two houses down from Beverly. Since I was on house arrest, at certain times I could leave the premises of the house. Tanya would always make sure I had everything I wanted such as alcohol and cigarettes.

She also had a brother named Mike who'd just gotten out of reform school. To no surprise, Mike and I became best friends. We would terrorize the neighborhood. A couple of weeks after knowing Mike, he introduced me to a guy called Peanut who was older than us but just as devious. Before long, Beverly started getting the word from the neighbors of the things Mike,

49

Peanut, and I were doing. Within a month of moving to Upper Marlboro, Maryland I had a new girlfriend and a new set of friends.

At the same time, I was beginning my new life, so was Diana. She was now about eight months pregnant and showing. I got so caught up in myself that I started neglecting the fact that I had a child on the way. My double life was soon about to be exposed again. I knew Diana and Tanya's work schedules so I always made time for both without the other one finding out.

Until one day, I had Diana come over. I didn't know that Tanya didn't go to work that day. She was able to look out her window and see the front of Beverly's house. Tanya did not accept my deceptive actions too well because before I knew it, she had come out of the house and started questioning me about the pregnant young lady I was conversing with.

Diana became extremely irritated by Tanya's interrogation and things quickly got out a hand. I was already walking on a thin line at Beverly's house and now there was a big confrontation between my soon to be child's mother and my girlfriend.

I ended the confrontation by cursing both young ladies out and demanding both to go home. Both Diana and Tanya went home but the damage was already done because the word about the incident had gotten back to

Beverly. I was now faced with another deadline to move with the baby on the way and the feeling of disappointment resurfacing from all these women in my life.

At this point, I was drinking every day. Alcohol seemed to be my only outlet that made me numb to the reality of the hell that I created for myself. One day I was drunk and cooking, which wasn't a good combination and almost burned down Beverly's house. That was the last straw she told me. I had to leave immediately after my house arrest sentence was over.

A couple of days before my house arrest sentence was over, my older sister Bridget said I could come live with her temporarily and she did mean TEMPORARILY. Everything was in harmony in Bridget's household for about the first two weeks. I met a guy named Tim who was mischievous and liked to drink like I did.

Soon things started to spiral out of control once again. Bridget was now into the church. I started coming into her house reeking of alcohol. I began to attract the same type of company that I attracted throughout my life so far, which were misled souls.

In a short period of time, I began to build a reputation in Bridget's neighborhood as a troublemaker. I used to hang out and drink at a laundromat with my new friends less than five minutes away from the complex Bridget lived in. The manager of the laundromat was a guy from New York named Jay that was about ten years older than me.

At the time, he would always tell me that he saw himself in me when he was my age. One day my drinking buddy Tim and I were hanging out at the laundromat, and I got into a huge disagreement and alcohol took over my emotions. Not thinking straight in broad daylight, I pulled out a gun and put it to Tim's head. We were in front of everyone in the laundromat and there were people walking by. By coincidence, someone knew my brother Pernell who was visiting Bridget that day and ran and got him. Pernell ran to where I was and talked me into giving him the gun.

Now Bridget was a 'one strike, you're out' type of person. She didn't believe in giving chances like Beverly did, so when she found out about the confrontation that happened in front of the laundromat, I had to evacuate her house immediately without any exception.

When Bridget kicked me out of her apartment, reality hit me like a ton of bricks. I finally realized I had burned all my bridges with my family members and had no place to go. The manager of the laundromat, Jay, would let me sleep in a room in the back of the laundromat whenever he had to work. Jay convinced his wife to let me stay with them a couple of nights and the last night he let me stay, he explained to me that if I didn't change my life I would have a fatherless child and end up dead or in jail. That was the last time I stayed over at Jay's house. Fortunately, he would still let me sleep and hang out at the laundromat.

Even though Bridget had kicked me out of her apartment, I still would just hang out around the neighborhood because I had met a lot of new friends. On this one particular day, I was hanging out drinking behind the laundromat, as usual, and this guy approached me and asked me if I knew where to get some smoke, meaning marijuana. Being that I knew most of the people in the neighborhood that were involved in illegal activities I connected him with someone I knew.

The more the guy and I conversed on the way to the man's house, the more we realized we had a lot in common. The guy introduced himself to me as Kofi but he said his nickname was Black. Black would bring new meaning to my life.

For the next couple of days, Black and I would meet behind the laundromat and converse. He would be smoking marijuana and I would be drinking a 40 ounce of beer. Black and I would discuss how I got kicked out of my sister's house and how I had nowhere to live. After I gained Blacks' trust, he said he wanted to introduce me to his cousin. He felt as though we had a lot in common. He explained to me that his cousin

53

liked to drink and had a reputation for taking no mess from anyone.

One day Black and I were hanging out and he decided to have his cousin join us in our daily ritual where he would smoke and I would drink and converse about the unfairness of the world. When I met Black's cousin there was an instant connection. We both liked the same things. We both preferred drinking and we had similar criminal backgrounds. He introduced himself as Na Na short for Kwamnon. Without even knowing Na Na for a day, it felt like we knew each other for a lifetime.

When I was discussing my current living situation, Na Na suggested that I could crash at his house for a little while. Na Na lived in Northeast Washington DC, in front of the dope strip with his father. Kofi and his older brother Yaw also known as Drunk lived there as well. I took Na Na up on his offer and started sleeping in his attic.

It was like a party - we would drink and chase neighborhood girls all day. The house became almost like a frat house with no rules because the house was three stories and Na Na's father lived in the basement and seldom came upstairs. When his father came upstairs, I would find a place to hide so he wouldn't see me. One day things didn't go as planned and his father

54

caught me asleep in the attic and asked me with his strong Ghanaian accent what I was doing in his house.

Na Na's father Kofi was a man who did not sugarcoat what he had to say. Before I could say anything, Na Na came to my defense and told his father my situation. Surprisingly Kofi was very understanding and told me I could live in the house as long as I followed his rules.

By his rules he meant to come down stairs every night at 8 o'clock for prayer and not to have women and alcohol in his house. But being that Kofi seldom left the basement except for work, his rules really didn't exist for Na Na and I.

As time went on, you could say that Kofi adopted me as his son because he would treat me the same as he would Na Na with no exceptions, fussing us both out with his strong accent about our mischief. He would always say, "I'm going to send you boys to Ghana so you can learn how to be men" and we would always laugh and continue our mischievous behavior once we were out of his presence.

After a month in the neighborhood, which some would consider the hood or a bad neighborhood, everybody from the dealers to the law-abiding citizens became family to me. We would all stand on the block to share alcohol, weed and converse about past street tales while making drug transactions. At all times, it would be 15 to 20 guys hanging out on that block at night, being loud. You would hear occasional gunshots which I soon became immune to.

Now looking back, I realize that we all were just kids that were lost, who found validation in each other. I hadn't felt a part of something like this since I was younger, attending the 4-H camp. Whenever I would leave outside of the neighborhood, I couldn't wait to get back to hang out with my new family on 22nd St.

Every day was a different adventure. If you had a problem with one person on that block you had a problem with everyone on that block so I felt safe in the confines of that section. If I was to have someone stop by to see me, they would have to call me first before driving down the street so I could inform everyone that a strange car would be coming through.

Now my life was starting to feel stable because I had Kofi as a father figure and a group of brothers that took care of one another. Eventually the time was coming closer to Diana giving birth to our child which I found out would be a girl. Diana and I began to rebuild our relationship in hopes of raising a family together.

On October 31, 1994, my life changed in an instant. I received a call that Diana was going into labor. As soon as I got the news I ran downstairs and told everyone on the block that I was about to become a father so everyone loaded up in their cars and followed me to the hospital. The waiting room at the hospital was in total chaos with 20 to 25 street dudes reeking of alcohol and weed being loud and disruptive and full of excitement.

Diana's mother walked into the waiting room in disbelief, stating that all these people couldn't be here and that some of them must leave because the hospital staff is complaining about the noise. Some of my brothers left and the ones that stayed behind lowered their tones and calmed down.

I was in the back while Diana went into labor. As soon as I saw the head of this little girl pop out, I immediately knew what unconditional love felt like. We named the girl Crystal after Diana's mother's best friend who passed away and Chanel as part of my first name Linel. I can not explain the joy I felt that day.

After the birth of Crystal my baby girl, the fellows and I went down to Georgetown to celebrate. The next day I shared the news of my newborn child with Kofi. He had a look of both happiness and seriousness at the same time. He stated to me that I had to be responsible because I had a child, meaning I had to find a job to take care of this child.

For once in my life, I felt as though I had to be responsible for someone other than myself. I was used to people being responsible for me. I decided to seriously look for a job and I finally found one at the mall.

The first day on the job, I went in to work happy about my fresh outlook on my new life, only to find out that my manager was Diana's oldest daughter's father.

I felt like the higher power was paying me back for all the wrong that I had done. The situation was extremely awkward. Every day I went to work, I died 1000 deaths inside because not only was this man my boss, but the situation also reminded me that Diana had a past.

That work arrangement lasted no longer than two weeks. Kofi was disappointed in my decision to quit the job and encouraged me to try to get it back. At this point, I felt like I'd rather take my chances in the street making money rather than constantly dying on the inside while taking orders from my child's step-sister's father. Going back to that job was not an option.

I don't think I even picked up the check that was owed to me for the two weeks I worked. In the midst of being at a crossroad in my life, now being 18 years old with no work experience and with a child to support, my drinking habit increased tremendously. Now I needed a 40 ounce beer in the morning as I started my day.

At this low time in my life, trying to live a legal life with no job, little money and a newborn baby, I was actually contemplating suicide. On this day, with my mind racing, a friend asked me to go to the mall with him. I hesitated because I had no interest in going to watch someone else spend money when I didn't have any myself. When we got to the mall, he went and purchased whatever item he came to the mall to obtain and as we walked to the car in the parking lot, I noticed a jacket on the ground.

It was a nice jacket and at the time I needed one. So, I looked around, didn't see anyone looking, so I picked up the jacket and proceeded to the car. Once in the car I tried on the jacket and it was a perfect fit. But I felt something in the pocket. I put my hand in the pocket to see what it was and it is a wad of hundred dollar bills.

I was trying not to disclose to the person I was riding with what I had just found because I knew he would've felt entitled to some of the money being that we went to the mall together.

At this point in time, I was excited and nervous, so I told him to speed up because someone may be looking for the jacket I found because it had a couple hundred dollars in it and I gave him $100 of it.

When we finally made it to the neighborhood, then of course he told me "thank you for the money" and I proceeded upstairs in the house. I went into the bathroom and locked the door and started counting the money I just found. It was close to $10,000. I no longer felt hopeless. I felt like the higher power gave me a break. I did what any street dude would do to double his money, I invested some of the money into drugs and put on Na Na and his older brother Drunk.

Doing the " right thing" was no longer in my thought process. I had converted back to my old ways of hustling, drinking and womanizing. The fact that I had a newborn didn't change my decision from taking chances in the streets in order to provide for my new responsibility. My past had once again resurfaced.

The business that I had invested in was short lived after someone stole my stash. In order for me to continue in business, I had to find a place where the street value of the product I had was double, to make up for the stash that was stolen from me. So, I made a few phone calls to a couple of friends I had back home in Sanford, North Carolina and they informed me it would be the perfect time for me to come down with the product because the town was in a drought.

I got a girl I had met a couple of days before the incident to rent me a car and being that my friends and I didn't have a license, I also needed her to drive my friends and myself to Sanford, North Carolina. The trip to Sanford was everything my friends over the phone told me it would be. I had sold out of the product within four hours of being in town. The trip made me appear to be the big man to my friends who came down with me from DC because I was the first person to take them out of the city.

My friends and I got back to DC and now it was business as usual. On this particular day, reality hit home and changed my mindset temporarily. Na Na and I were sitting upstairs in the house and we heard gunshots which wasn't anything out of the ordinary until we heard people screaming and yelling. So, he ran downstairs and got outside only to see Na Na's older brother Drunk shot on the ground, bleeding from both his legs. Thankfully Drunk recovered from the gunshot wounds but I can only think that it easily could've been me laying on that ground.

5   DOING THE SAME THINGS EXPECTING A DIFFERENT RESULT

Shortly after that incident, with Na Na's older brother Drunk getting shot in front of the house, I decided to move out on my own and Diana was excited about my decision and began assisting me in finding a place. My daughter's babysitter had a house that she was renting rooms from. The house was located in Landover, Maryland, a part of the city known as Kent Land. Eventually I decided to take the place with the thought that Maryland had to be a slower kind of pace than the part of DC I was relocating from.

The assumption I had was wrong because the first week after moving to Landover, I walked outside one morning only to see a dead body lying in the driveway directly across the street from the house that I was living in. People on that street must have been immune to the violence that occurred in my *now* new neighborhood. In DC, I experienced and had seen a lot of violence but it was different because I knew most of the perpetrators. I began to adjust to my new neighborhood and in the process started meeting people.

To pay my rent I still was traveling to my old neighborhood daily to sell drugs. After a couple months, my trips to DC slowed down and the guys around the neighborhood became okay with me hustling on the block as long as I didn't overstep their boundaries. As months passed, the communication between my family that adopted me in DC soon became nonexistent.

I now had a new street family in Landover but the bond was not the same as the bond I had with my street family in DC. I was always hesitant and never felt completely safe in my new environment. My relationship with Diana began to grow stronger as my daughter grew older. At home Diana was starting to get a lot of slack from her mother for continuously dealing with me. At this point Diana was ready to move out of her mother's house in order to be with me and raise a family.

I decided to make one more attempt at leaving the street life alone so once again I looked for a job. Finally I found a job with a temp agency. One of the jobs that the agency referred me to gave me a permanent position. The job was easy. It was in a big warehouse that stored files of all sorts and my job was to pull the files upon request. For once I got a taste of what normal felt like. When the company hired me permanently they gave me a uniform. I wore that uniform everywhere after work for the first couple weeks. It gave me a sense of pride that I had never felt.

Not only Diana, but my family was extremely excited to see me work in a legal job. Honestly, I never really had to let go of my illegal job, it just turned into a side hustle. I was now leading a double life working a legal job during the day and working my illegal job at night. By then, living a double life was second nature to me. Diana felt as though I had turned into the man that she wanted me to be.

After I worked steadily at the job for six months, Diana suggested that we move in together and begin raising our daughter. Diana and I found an apartment in Landover, Maryland and we moved in together. Life with Diana and two daughters,started feeling perfect to me. I was working a job every day, coming home to my family and having family outings.

The whole family thing would've probably worked if I would have left my old habits of drinking and being promiscuous in the past. My past always resurfaced as I began staying out at night and choosing to stay at home and drink instead of going on family outings. Shortly after my daughter turned one year old, Diana had another surprise that she was pregnant again. By this time my cheating was out of control, to the point where girls would call the house and ask for me.

I recall one time, I wanted Diana out of the house so I acted as though I had seen a mouse in the kitchen because I knew her fear of mice. So she agreed to stay at her mother's house until I killed it but the truth was I just wanted her to go so I could invite another young lady over to the house to have intercourse.

I believe Diana put up with my cheating ways in hopes that I would change. The day came when Diana had reached a point where she told me that once her pregnancy was over, she was going to leave me. I did not believe her because she would always threaten to leave me and never left. When Diana was going through labor with my second child I showed up late and under the influence of alcohol. Diana had given birth to another girl which we named Lynette Betty Ann after her grandmother. That day in the hospital I had told Diana I was going to do right by her and stop the cheating. It was too late.

The day after she came home with our little girl, I was up to my old tricks staying out all night. This time when I pulled up to the apartment, I saw a U-Haul truck. As I walked towards the apartment I saw Diana's friend and her uncle carrying bags towards the truck. When I walked into the apartment which was now empty, I saw Diana in tears shaking her head as I walked towards her. Out of nowhere, with all her built-up anger, she began crying, punching and kicking me, telling me to get out until she finished moving because she didn't want to see my face.

Eventually, I lost the apartment, quit my job and ended up doing what I knew best. My brother Pernell offered and insisted that I come live with him until I got my own place. Pernell and I got along great up until I started to drink. Pernell and I would have the most fun together chasing women and partying. He was the ideal big brother. His only concern was my over-the-top drinking habit. While Pernell would wake up and go to work in the morning, I would wake up and go to the liquor store.

I would always tell him that I was out looking for work all that day while in actuality, I was chasing women and getting drunk.. To make my current situation worse, I would invite friends over and totally disregard any rules he set in his household. I know that I was severely depressed at that point in time and was self medicating with alcohol and should have been seeking some professional help. I felt dead inside.

Diana would not communicate with me and I couldn't see my daughters and on top of that, Pernell was starting to lose his patience with me. He gave me a timeline to move out of his apartment. I resorted back to the one thing that made me feel empowered, women.

I had become so manipulative of women that I could meet a woman that day and she would be giving me her body by the end of that day.

In a strange way, my promiscuous lifestyle gave me a false sense of control because I felt as though I had no control over my real life. Being able to convince a woman to share an intimate moment with me was powerful in my own bubble of the world I had built for myself.

The problem became worse once I started to develop a conscience and the feelings I experienced as empowerment, started to slowly shift to feelings of guilt. However, that didn't slow down my womanizing. I was taking advantage of women's gullibility which only increased my depression.

That year I could not control my drinking or the chaos I considered to be drunken rages. One drunken night, I finally pushed Pernell to his limit and he kicked me out of his home. Honestly, I was surprised that Pernell put up with my antics for such a long period of time. My drunken behavior landed me back on the streets, homeless and staying with whoever would let me stay at their house for a couple of days.

I was a full-fledged alcoholic and it was only a matter of time before I would self-destruct. I was in a real dark space in my life and didn't care if I lived or died. I started taking out my anger verbally on the women around me to make them feel the pain that I was feeling. I felt like the women were using me for sex and that justified my behavior.

In the midst of all the chaos and dysfunction that was going on in my life, a friend of mine introduced me to a guy that would help me financially from that day forward. The guy he introduced me to had a 745 BMW and was draped in designer clothing and spoke with a foreign, sort of Jamaican accent. The first impression I got of the guy that I soon would know as Dre, was that he was doing good for himself in the dope game but later I would find out my perception was wrong.

Dre explained to me the details of the hustle that he wanted me to partake in and explained that if I hustled hard I would make more money than I ever did selling drugs while taking less risk of incarceration. I was optimistic because what he was telling me seemed too good to be true but I decided to take the chance because I had nothing to lose and frankly just didn't care.

Dre informed me that to make this scheme happen, I would need to recruit people. I had no problem with recruiting people because the women that I was dealing with believed anything that I would tell them. Being that I was a little unsure of Dres' scheme, I chose to use a lady I had just met as my test subject. I knew if things went wrong, she could not trace it back to me.

I convinced the lady to go along with my plan and assured her of the payoff. Dre provided me with the documentation I needed to give to the young lady and explained to me the breakdown of the money once the transaction was completed. I relayed the information that was given to me as though I was a pro and only reminded the young lady of the payoff.

The payoff if successful, would be more than I would have made selling drugs in a couple of months but I remained unfazed by the numbers when conversing with Dre. Now the moment of truth arrived and the young lady walked into the institution with confidence because of how easy I told her the transaction would be. I was extremely nervous on the inside because I honestly had no idea how this scheme would work.

Every time I would hear a noise or see a police car while we were waiting my heart would almost beat out of my chest. The wait was intense the first two minutes she was in the financial institution. It felt like two hours had passed. As I started to lose faith in Dre's white collar scheme, the young lady walked out of the financial institution, smiling. The young lady then got in the car and handed me the envelope full of money and then I handed it to Dre to give the young lady her cut, which was much less than mine. Dre would settle with me after we dropped her off.

The young lady was excited over what she was paid. I also had to remain calm as though I had dealt with large amounts of money before. Dre and I dropped off the young lady, then he handed me three grand. I acted as though I was disappointed but I was more excited on the inside than the young lady displayed on the outside.

I felt like I was in a dream and that someone would wake me up soon because I couldn't believe that I had made $3000 in less than 30 minutes. The first thing I did was get a hotel room because I didn't have a place to stay. I got a couple of new outfits and went to the liquor store and celebrated my new career. I felt as though I found the hustle that I was good at doing other than selling drugs. Now I was becoming Dre's number one man because I had no shortage of recruits, especially females. I began to slowly move out of a dark space in my life and started covering up my depression and insecurities with material items.

The hotel I was at became my permanent residence at the time. The manager also became impressed with the different women I would have over. I had plenty of money, a nice car and the appearance of a big-time drug dealer. I began to shop daily at the mall which was located directly across the street from the hotel that I was living in Carrollton, Maryland.

I now know and understand for a fact that the energy you give off is the energy you attract because I ran into an associate of mine whom I knew as James from the apartment complex Pernell used to live. James and I used to hang out and drink together while we reminisced about the past. I discovered that he was in the same business as Dre and I so we would later link up.

Now that I look back I think about the odds of me meeting someone from my past that was involved in the same exact white collar scheme. That wasn't a coincidince. Eventually, my old associate James and I began doing business because by then I was no longer an amateur and had less recruits to go around. Now I had two sources of income coming in and started purchasing whatever I liked. I started giving money to Diana for my girls and she began hesitantly communicating with me and occasionally let me see my kids.

With this steady flow of new found wealth came an ego. Before, when I used to drink, I would be a little disruptive. But that had come to an end and now I became a violent, arrogant drunk who bragged about the women he conquered and the money he was making while being confrontational with anyone who

71

disagreed with my nonsense. My ego had gotten so big that Dre no longer wanted to work with me because he feared that my reckless behavior would bring unnecessary attention to what he was involved in. That was okay with me because I was still making money with James on the side.

With James being the only person I was working with now, I was ready to go all out because I had to supplement the money that I was making with Dre. One day James came to pick me up to conduct business as usual but he had another guy in the car with him. I wasn't feeling that because I didn't need any extra people knowing my business nor knowing all the people that I recruited.

Hanging out with my boys. Me, my ego and a sawed off pump shotgun in my mouth

Looking at the dude I asked James, "What is he here for?" Tension got tight in the car when I asked that question because the dude looked at me with a mean mug as James ordered him to calm down and introduced the guy as Frank, his partner. Now things became really awkward and Frank and I began to exchange cheap shots at each other which turned to the point of everything becoming almost physical. James intervened and reminded us that it's all about the money and we fairly can get what we deserve and more.

I wasn't feeling his partner because he was just as arrogant and disrespectful as me. Eventually we both came to the realization that we had to work together to keep living the lifestyles we were growing accustomed to, such as shopping and partying hard. Once all the differences between Frank and myself were settled, the three of us operated like a corporation.

Everyone knew their position which eliminated confusion. During the weekdays, we would meet up no later than 10 o'clock every morning to check on our investments and to discuss plans for the new recruits for our white collar scheme. The three of us grew into a bond of brothers; we had each other's back no matter the situation. If you had a problem with one of us, you had a problem with all three of us. The three of us were so connected we even created our own language that only we could decode when we would conduct business around recruits or people that weren't in our circle.

I felt completely free and I felt I could be myself without fear of judgment. I was around two people that seemed to understand my pain. I would be lying if I said that the first three to four years of doing business with James and Frank weren't the most adventurous fun times of my life. We all had plenty of money, decent cars and countless parties with plenty of women, with just the three of us as the host.

We were living life so fast, that I did not realize how my drinking habit had increased and so did my depression. After a while, the money was no longer filling the void. I had mixed feelings because I was happy to finally have a true connection and money, but due to my past, I was always scared that any day what I considered happiness would come to an end. Eventually, instead of all three of us meeting up in the mornings, it began to be just me and Frank meeting in the morning.

We had a designated spot to meet every morning on the stoop of the apartments Pernell lived in because there were always a lot of girls walking to the subway on their way to work or school in the mornings and we enjoyed the view on some days as the reward. This guy that I could not stand when I first met him had now become my best friend. James was more responsible than the both of us and did not participate in our risky carefree lifestyle. While we would be out spending money, James would be at home saving his money, which in the long run would benefit all of us. I would soon find out that you get what you pay for, including women.

One day, Frank and I were hanging out riding around on one of our missions drinking and smoking when I spotted this young lady with a body like a ghetto goddess. Her walk showed confidence like she was the bomb and she caught my attention. When we pulled up on her, she rolled her eyes at us and kept walking which was an instant turn on for me because I wasn't used to rejection.

I got in the car and chased her down and convinced her to stop and talk to me. After about 10 minutes of conversation, we exchanged numbers and I must admit that the whole day, I had the young lady that introduced herself as simply Keisha on my mind. I didn't want to seem desperate so I promised myself I would wait a week before giving Keisha a call but to my surprise she called me a day later.

My first conversation with Keisha lasted at least an hour. After the first call, we conversed at least two other times after that. Keisha and I appeared to have a lot in common and we made plans to see each other that next day.

The next day, when we hooked up, I invited her to the hotel I was living in. She appeared to be impressed because it was a nice hotel I was living in at that time and I had told the manager whom I was cool with that I had a special date. He hooked me up with the Jacuzzi room and Keisha ended up staying two days with me.

I began to let Keisha stay in my room some days while I would be out conducting business with James and Frank. I was no longer hanging out with Frank daily. I started spending all my free time with my new girlfriend. Now that I look back at that point in time in my life, I realize that I had no business with a girlfriend being that I was an alcoholic, depressed, womanizer. I know for a fact that money makes people ignore a lot of things that are obvious.

Keisha and I began to move fast and within a month she convinced me that we should move in together. I was extremely hesitant, because I remembered the after effects of Diana and I living together and I wasn't ready to go on that emotional roller coaster again. Eventually, I agreed and we moved to Landover, Maryland, to a neighborhood that was rough but not nowhere near as rough as the neighborhood I lived in previously.

Meanwhile, business was still going pretty good and I was no longer just shopping for myself. I had taken on a new responsibility, Keisha. I began spending money as soon as I got it and James and Frank became concerned about my irresponsibility with money but I would ignore them. Eventually, our business began to slow down because financial institutions began to catch on to the scheme we were involved in.

When the money slowed down, my relationship with Keisha took a turn for the worse. What I considered to be the ideal relationship became a living nightmare with constant arguments over money and my drinking habit, which was never an issue to her in the past. My old behaviors returned but one day things changed during a typical argument. I lost total control of myself and began punching and kicking Keisha.

After the altercation, I snapped back out of my rage and saw the damage that I had done to the woman I supposedly loved. I felt guilty and ashamed. I promised myself and Keisha that I would never lift my hand to hit her again which eventually turned out to be a lie. The abuse seemed to be consistent with every time I would get drunk and that was almost daily.

I would have feelings of worthlessness and self guilt and would blame Keisha for my financial decline because I felt as though our relationship was built on material things and that if I completely went broke she would end up leaving me anyway. Keisha must have been just as lost as I was to tolerate my physical and verbal abuse. To no surprise, our relationship was falling apart; business was going downhill in the area we lived in so we had to journey outside of the area to generate money to maintain our lifestyles.

I contacted a couple of friends I grew up with in North Carolina and explained to them the financial benefits of the white collar scheme that my partners and I had going on and within a couple weeks after our conversation, my friends back home in North Carolina had found me some recruits for our scheme.

After I shared the good news with James and Frank, we put a plan in motion so we could set up shop as discreetly as possible when we started conducting business in a town that they were unfamiliar with. The first thing we decided on was getting a rental car, something low-key to make the trip out of town but none of us had access or our owned credit cards because we always dealt with cash.

Even though I was in a serious relationship with Keisha, I had a corporate, older, married woman on the side named Jenelle, who had the credentials to make that happen. Jenelle was a college-educated, powerful and extremely successful black woman in the corporate world. My relationship with Jenelle was solely built on adventurous sex and hour long conversations on how boring her life had become with her husband.

I recalled one of the times I met Jenelle on her lunch break, at a park with a golf course. We had sex in broad daylight on the green. Another memorable time was in the park on top of my car and we got caught by the police but the officer let us go with a warning. Jenelle was a rider with no strings attached, who had no problem doing what I asked of her, so when I asked her to rent me a car, it was not a problem at all. We had transportation now and we had to find a way to get the documentation we needed to the North Carolina recruits once we got there, which was the most important part.

Eventually, we got everything organized and ready to go. I asked Keisha to drive us because she had a legitimate license and it would give more of the perception of a family trip if we'd gotten pulled over. We made it to North Carolina safely, but had a small delay. We were told that the documentation we needed would arrive the next day, but it didn't.

The documentation we needed, came two days later than scheduled, but it was well worth the wait because every single transaction was successful and we found a new area to conduct business. Even though things appeared to look better businesswise, my relationship with Keisha continued to deteriorate and money could not make up for the verbal and physical abuse I had been doing to her.

The trip to North Carolina was a success and on the way back to Maryland, the guys and I began planning our next trip with excitement. Finally back home, I assumed that since business had picked up, it would keep my relationship with Keisha from breaking up. For some reason or another Keisha decided to look in the glove compartment of the rental car, I guess out of curiosity to see who rented me the car. When she realized that Jenelle had rented me the car, any chance of us reconciling was out of the question because when Keisha and I first began our relationship, I had told her about my relationship with Jenelle. Plus they had gotten into it over the phone a couple of times in the past with Jenelle calling on my phone being disrespectful to her.

I lied to Keisha by telling her that I had cut off all communication with Jenelle. I continued seeing Jenelle at least once a week. After I dropped off the car at the rental company, the ride back home was completely quiet. Once we got to our house, things exploded. Keisha called me every name under the sun and began to throw things at me while she cursed me out.

In the midst of the commotion, I went to grab her and somehow my hand missed her arm and hit her face. Out of all the times Keisha and I had gotten into altercations, she never would let the authorities get involved but this time she did. The cops arrived and she explained to them with a bleeding mouth, that she

81

did not want to press charges on me, she just wanted me to leave the house.

But it wasn't that easy because the cops ran my name and I had a couple outstanding warrants in DC, so it was impossible for the police not to take me to jail. Once I got the opportunity to make my first phone call from jail, I called Diana because she had the only phone number I could remember. Diana didn't give me the negative response I expected. She seemed to be kind of relieved to hear my voice, even though I was incarcerated.

She began helping me find out information about my case and would come see me on visitation day and put money on my books. At times when I was alone in my cell, I would feel guilty knowing that I did not deserve the help she was giving me due to the way I had treated her in the past. Diana would make three-way calls to James and Frank to keep them updated with my case, being that I had no bond or definite court date and I was the connection to the North Carolina recruits that we had just started doing business with.

Four months had passed, and I finally received a court date in two months from that date. On the upside, my relationship with Diana had blossomed and she showed her love with her actions such as never missing a visit or phone call. I did what they call jailhouse talk. During our conversations, I would convince her that I was going to do right by her and my daughters when I got out and that I was going to stop drinking and cheating which was easy to say being that I was in a controlled environment.

Diana even went as far as making arrangements for us to live together upon my release. She had no clue I was in an almost two-year relationship prior to me getting incarcerated but she would soon find out in an unexpected way. As usual, on visitation, I received a call to the visitation room only to see Keisha and not Diana. I was surprised and confused. Keisha had appeared to have lost weight and when our eyes connected she gave me a blank smile.

I sat down and spoke to her. She responded with a mumble and a tear slid down her cheek. That's when I noticed the wire around her teeth when she smiled that didn't look like braces and when she continued to speak I noticed that she didn't open her mouth fully. I finally got the courage to ask her what happened to her face in a concerned tone, only to find out that I had broken her jaw during the last altercation we had gotten in, which led to me getting incarcerated.

I felt like I wanted to die, knowing that I had caused this young lady that much physical pain and to this day I don't understand why she didn't press legal charges on my sorry ass. All that went through my mind at that time was, I must have been wrong about Keisha thinking she was with me for financial gain but in actuality the whole time she really did love me. I was unable to recognize love because I had no clue what real love felt like other than the birth of my daughters.

When reality hit me about what I had done to this young lady, I couldn't hold back the tears and cried like a baby the rest of the visit. After my visit with Keisha, I felt numb and less of a man. I stayed in my cell for two days after that, not making phone calls to Diana. I just waddled in my self-pity. I finally accepted the fact that my drinking was completely out of control and how my actions when under the influence of alcohol could easily affect someone else's life.

I started communicating with Diana again and discussing with her how I was a changed man and wanted to be with her and my kids as a family but I knew inside I was saying that out of guilt because I knew I did not deserve the support she was giving me while I was incarcerated. The moment of truth finally arrived which was my release date.

I was excited and unsure at the same time because it's easy to say I changed when I was in a   controlled environment. Diana had made arrangements for me to move in with her and my girls upon my release which seemed like a good idea at the time. I had no place else to go due to the confrontation that Keisha and I had that led to my incarceration. When I walked out of Upper

Marlboro Detention Center I was greeted by my friend and neighbor, Rock.

Rock and I were like brothers. We made a lot of money together and he was one of the few people I would converse with while I was incarcerated. Rock greeted me with a smile and appeared to be full of excitement. He told me to look into the glove compartment of his car. As soon as I opened the glove compartment, I saw the demon that I was trying to avoid which was alcohol looking me straight in the face.

I wanted to decline the invitation but of course I didn't. As a surprise, Rock had gotten me a half pint of Hennessy and a pack of cigarettes, two habits I told Diana I had given up. Within a few minutes after being released I had picked up where I left off. I hadn't changed my old ways at all, they were just prolonged.

Rock took me to his house which was directly across the hall from my old apartment with Keisha. Rock filled me in to all the people who were going in and out of my old house in the latest neighborhood gossip. To my surprise, Keisha wasn't seeing anyone to his knowledge and would always ask him about me while I was incarcerated.

I explained to Rock how I reestablished my relationship with Diana and how I planned on being a family man. He just looked at me and shook his head and laughed as though I was joking. I called Diana while she was at work to get the address to her new home. Diana seemed to be overly excited knowing that I was released and wanted to put our family back together, so she thought. Rock and I had a couple more drinks to celebrate my release until it was time for me to meet Diana at her house.

I got to Diana's house reeking of alcohol and cigarette smoke, smelling like all the elements I had told her I would no longer indulge in. She told me to come in and looked at me as though she had been defeated by the things I was telling her while I was incarcerated. That day was the first-time Diana had ever given me eye contact and told me she was finished dealing with me but I could stay with her a couple weeks until I found a place of my own.

I didn't even last a week in Diana's house because the drinking increased and the disrespect with other women resurfaced and she stated to me that she wasn't going to have that type of behavior around our kids; I had to leave.

Rock agreed to let me stay with him and his wife but that didn't work out long because his wife began hinting that I was a bad influence on her husband. .

86

One day I was leaving Rock's apartment and Keisha was in the hallway. We spoke to each other hesitantly and started a conversation about how the situation in the past could've been handled differently and to my surprise after I apologized for my actions, she apologized to me as well which made the situation even more awkward because I knew that there was nothing she could have done that could have provoked the way I behaved that night.

At the end of the conversation, she invited me to dinner the following night and I accepted the offer. I arrived at the home which we once shared and had feelings of emptiness and guilt that night. The feelings of that night somehow reemerged in me emotionally. After dinner, Keisha discussed with me her interest in rekindling our prior relationship which led up to an intimate moment between us.

While we lay in the bed, Keisha asked if I was willing to work on rebuilding our relationship. My mind and my heart said yes. However, the words that came out became the best decision I made for us. I knew I could not pretend as though the incident that led up to her jaw breaking didn't happen. So, for once in my life, I made a selfless decision to sacrifice my feelings and desires for the well-being and safety of a woman.

I could only see my life spiraling out of control at a fast rate. I had no place to live, I had burnt all my bridges with family members and there were limitations on seeing my daughters. I also realized I had created all of these situations. In the midst of my life falling apart at a fast rate, I reconnected with my partners in crime James and Frank. They were the only positive force I had in my life. They supplied me with money and provided me with a place to stay, the hotel. The hotel stay became extremely expensive after a couple of months. I no longer had the connections for hotel rooms.

Since I had a connection in North Carolina for our scheme, I thought relocating there would be more lucrative for us and would be more stable for me. Once again I was faced with a difficult decision. I was tired of my past resurfacing and having to rebuild my life.

6 THE CALM BEFORE THE STORM – HITTING ROCK BOTTOM

I called around to family members and friends that lived in North Carolina to find a place to temporarily live and to my surprise, my father, Linel agreed to let me move in with him. We had the agreement that I would need to find a place of my own. He required that I also wait three weeks before I could move in because he had to discuss the living situation with his wife. I had three weeks to save money before my move to North Carolina.

As usual, I found a vulnerable young lady I had dealt with in the past named Tee. My deceptive ways were in gear because I knew that she wanted to be in a committed relationship. I decided to capitalize off of her emotions and convinced her that I too wanted to be in a committed relationship. I confided in her by sharing that I was in an unstable living situation and needed somewhere to stay. I had no plans on being in a serious relationship. My plans were to leave Washington DC within a couple weeks.

She agreed to let me move in but the only problem was, she lived with her mother and her mother was a

Christian lady who did not believe in a man living with a woman while not married. Tee believed everything that I told her. She secretly moved me in against her mother's wishes. Tee's room was in the basement of the house which she shared with her brother. Her mother rarely came to the basement but if someone decided to come to her room, she had a hiding place for me.

Throughout the day, I would be conducting business and at night I would be living in Tee's basement. Living a double life was nothing new to me. I was used to deceiving people to get what I wanted. I would discuss with Tee our plans of building a future together while planning transportation and living arrangements in North Carolina throughout the day.

I had reconnected with a cousin who lived in Washington, DC that just so happened to be going to North Carolina on the date that I was supposed to arrive. He agreed to let me ride with him and his family. He insisted, saying it would be foolish for me to spend money on a trip going to the same place. As the time got closer for me to leave, I packed and moved my clothes little by little, so it wouldn't be noticeable to Tee.

The day before I planned to leave, I hung out with Tee and further discussed our future together. I was just telling her what I thought she wanted to hear with no regards for her feelings. The day I was leaving, I made sure that Tee wasn't at home, I moved my clothes out of her room to permanently relocate to North Carolina. Everything went as planned. I had saved money and found a place to temporarily live and had a way to my destination. I felt guilty. I deceived someone who jeopardized her relationship with her family to accommodate me.

I felt so shameful on the ride to North Carolina that I said very little words. I would ignore Tee's calls because she was calling me and leaving back to back messages. She was crying, asking me to please call her because she didn't understand what could've gone wrong with our relationship. I never answered and eventually the messages she would leave turned into anger and rage; cursing and wishing that I would feel the hurt that she felt one day. Tees' wish would eventually come true because Karma is real and every bad seed that I planted would soon harvest within me and manifest in my life.

I finally got settled in North Carolina. I was in contact with my business partners so we could continue to work. Frank and James were making trips twice a month to collect money and drop off documents. Business was booming until greed began to play a factor. James began calling me asking me about how much money was Frank supposed to be bringing back and when James would make trips by himself Frank would ask the same questions about him but I had no complaints because both were giving me hush money to disclose the amount that they wanted me to.

This business practice went on for about a month until the trust was no longer amongst the three of us. I guess there is really no honor amongst thieves. Eventually, the trips started to become once every two months and at the rate I was spending money, partying and shopping, my money flow was decreasing extremely fast so I went back to the hustle that I knew, selling drugs.

I began investing the money that I was making with James and Frank in drugs to sell. One night after I re-upped on my drug supply, I was on my way home to Linel's house and to my surprise, there was a roadblock in front of his house. I had no license, had drugs and a gun in the car so my first instinct was to back up, but it was too late.

The officer flagged me to pull up and once the officer asked me for my license and registration, I knew if he found what I had in the car I would be going to jail. I was overly polite and responded with "yes sir, no sir" to every question he asked me. At one point I felt like he would just give me a ticket but that didn't happen. He asked me to step out of the car. When I stepped out my first instinct was to run but I was paralyzed by the fear of being shot in the back while trying to flee.

The officers searched the car and yelled "bingo" to the other officers that were on the scene as if he had already known what I had in the car. Apparently, I was the guy who they had set the roadblock for so they took me to jail even though I denied that the drugs or the gun was mine. The worst part is that it happened in front of Linel's house and it was only a matter of time before the news got back to him that his son had got locked up for possession of drugs and a firearm.

The next day I had my first appearance in court and my bond was set. I had a young lady that I had just met named Tee Tee to contact James and Frank so that they could possibly post bail so I could be released out of jail. My bail was posted and when I walked out of the correctional facility, I saw the young lady that had been making phone calls for me while I was incarcerated standing and smiling with James and Frank.

James and Frank explained to me that they could have gotten me out sooner but none of my family members or so-called friends would sign my bond but the young lady I had just met signed the bond for me. The first thought I had about Tee Tee was that she was a keeper because she just put her name on a bond and barely knew me. The first day of my release, I got back home to Linel's house only to see a note that read I was no longer welcome in his home and to leave the house key he gave me on the counter. History again repeated itself. Another incident caused the domino effect in my life.

Once again, I was forced to rebuild because I had invested all the money I had into drugs to sell and I was no longer welcomed at Linel's house where I was living. I explained to Tee Tee my living situation with Linel, kicking me out of his house and how I lost every cent I had when I got busted. She was the only person I knew in town that I felt comfortable talking to about my personal issues.

Tee Tee insisted that I move in with her to get back on my feet, which seemed to be a good idea at the time but in the long run turned out to be Karma catching up with me. I accepted the offer being that I had very little options so I decided to move in with Tee Tee and her two kids. Tee Tee had a daughter that was six years old and a son that was turning one year old which should've been a red flag to me that a woman would move a guy in, she had known less than two months. But to be honest, I was just happy to have somewhere to stay.

The first couple of weeks were good because business started back as usual, but this time it was short lived. The trust amongst James and Frank was completely gone so business came to a halt abruptly.

94

Now the only hustle that I was good at it came to an end. The money I had saved was completely gone and I was in a situation where I lived with a woman that I barely knew and had two little kids. The living situation which was cool at once now turned complicated.

I began hearing rumors about how Tee Tee was known around town for being promiscuous; something that I wouldn't have known being that I was new to the town. I would ignore the different stories I would hear because all I knew is that when I got into a difficult situation she was the only person that helped me and I respected her for that.

For about a month I absolutely had no money. I had to pawn a lot of my possessions to keep up my appearance and to help Tee Tee financially since I was living in her house. Energy truly attracts people with the same energy because while I was out one day I ran into an old friend that I knew from school named Tim.

Tim was known for his scams and flamboyant way of dressing. When I first saw Tim since we were in middle school, he appeared to look as if he was now living an alternative lifestyle which was no surprise to me or people that knew him. Tim and I talked and discussed the scam that he was into but I had little interest because what he was doing wasn't in my lane.

95

I felt comfortable talking to Tim so I explained to him the scam that my partners and I had going on up until a month ago. By the time I finished explaining the scheme that I was involved in to Tim, he informed me with excitement in his voice that he had a friend that lived about 30 minutes from the town I was living in that he wanted to introduce me to.

Tim and I exchanged contact information and he told me that he would arrange it so I could meet the guy that was involved in the business that I was previously involved in. Running into Tim couldn't have come at a better time because the tension between Tee Tee and I continued to grow because of my lack of finances. A couple of days after the meeting, Tim contacted me and told me that the guy was ready to meet with me. The meeting I had with the guy would be life changing. Tim agreed to pick me up because I had no car at the time since the police confiscated my car during the drug bust and I didn't have the money to get it out of the impoundment.

On the ride to Tim's friend's house, I was extremely quiet. A lot was riding on this connection. I needed it to be successful and lucrative. Tim and I arrived at Damon's house. After the formal introductions, we started discussing business. The more Damon described the scheme that he had going on, the more I realized that it was the same scheme I was previously involved

96

in with James and Frank. This scheme was on a smaller scale. I no longer had to divide the money. I was now connected to the source. Damon and I began doing business immediately following our meeting.

Now that money was coming in, the tension between Tee Tee and I began to decrease. I purchased a car that I saw at the dealership on my first trip to Damon's house. It was a white limited-edition Fleetwood Cadillac with a midnight blue leather interior. I told Tim that I was going to get that Cadillac even though at the time I told him I didn't have a pot to piss in or window to throw it out. I spoke it into existence because less than a month after telling him I was going to purchase that car I actually did.

That's when I learned how powerful words are. I began providing for the household that I was living in. I was partying, taking limos to the clubs; just enjoying life. The relationship between Tee Tee, her two kids and I began to blossom while at the same time my relationship with Diana and my two biological kids became nonexistent. I became so consumed with satisfying the needs of Tee Tee and her kids that I neglected the responsibility of my blood line.

Business with Damon and myself was consistent and lucrative but it would soon come to an end when the problems that I was running from would catch up with me mentally. I was self-medicating with alcohol at a rate higher than in the past. I would drink from the time I would wake up until it was time for me to go to bed. I would isolate myself from everyone and turn out all the lights and just cry for no reason which now I know that I was having a mental breakdown. The point came when I could no longer hide I had a mental illness.

I was a person that took pride in my appearance but now my appearance no longer seemed to matter. I could no longer conduct business because my anxiety would not let me be around a lot of different people and I needed people to conduct business. Tee Tee started noticing the drastic change in my behavior but I was good at masking my mental illness because that was something I had covered up most my life.

One day Tee Tee walked in on me while I was having a mental breakdown and I was forced to tell her about my past bouts with mental illness. Tee Tee appeared to be a little confused when I told her about my mental issues. Tee Tee advised me that if I wanted to continue to stay in her household, I would have to get some type of help since I was around her kids. I took Tee Tee's advice and went to the local mental health office and they referred me to several programs and prescribed me different medications.

I couldn't continue working with Damon at the time to generate income because of my anxiety around different people but I knew that I had to generate some sort of income since I was living at a young lady's house that had two kids she had to support.

The relationship between Tee Tee and I became extremely dysfunctional. She became very disrespectful towards me, as women in my past did and she would call me names like 'crazy' due to my mental illness.

The symptoms of my mental illness began to increase and so did my drinking which was already over the top. To make matters worse, I was taking prescription medication while drinking alcohol which was a toxic combination. The relationship got to the point where Tee Tee would kick me out of her house at least once a week. Through all the chaos, on a good note, one of the agencies that the mental health office referred me to hired people with mental illnesses like me.

The job paid very little money but at that time I had little to no money so I accepted the offer. The agency had a van that would pick up the employees and take them to work. A lot of the employees could not drive due to their mental illness. The job was extremely easy. All we did was look over metal plates sent over by different companies.

Failure's Not an Option

NORTH CAROLINA DIVISION OF MENTAL
HEALTH/DEVELOPMENTAL DISABILITIES/
SUBSTANCE ABUSE SERVICES

Dorothea Dix Hospital
Raleigh, North Carolina

DDH   MEDICAL

1-04-62-45
WINGATE, LINEL D.
12-28-2004   WAKE
BM 08-06-1975

DIAGNOSTIC STUDIES:

Electrocardiogram: Normal sinus rhythm at 66 and left ventricular hypertrophy by voltage.

TST STATUS:

Unknown.

COURSE IN HOSPITAL:

Problem #1. Hypotension with bradycardia: The patient was admitted to the Medical Unit and placed on telemetry for > 24 hours which revealed no events. It is suspected that the episode of hypotension and bradycardia are secondary to a vasovagal event and/or medicinal side effect after the patient received the new dose of Geodon. His Geodon was held and he was placed on intravenous fluids for intravascular dehydration. The was ruled out for sources of infection with the laboratory as reported above. Per psychiatry, the patient was re-started on Geodon during admission. He tolerated the re-addition without problem and his vital signs remained stable.

Problem #2. Dehydration: The patient was noticed to have intravascular dehydration evidenced by an elevated bicarbonate and elevated hemoglobin and hematocrit. The patient received intravenous fluids during admission and his laboratory values corrected. His creatinine was also elevated on admission at 1.3; however, after receiving intravenous fluids, it decreased to 0.9.

Problem #3. Recent left wrist laceration: the patient was continued on his pre-admission dose of Kellex and received dry dressing changes with triple antibiotic ointment during admission.

PSYCHIATRIC DIAGNOSIS:

Major Depressive Disorder with history of psychosis.

ADMITTING DIAGNOSIS:
Hypotension with bradycardia.

PRINCIPAL PHYSICAL DIAGNOSIS:
Vasovagal episode versus medicinal effect.

Page 3

Form No. DMH 1-25-03 (A-2)   DISCHARGE SUMMARY

One day while on break at the job, a staff member came outside to the break section where the employees could smoke a cigarette. The staff member was an extremely attractive young lady who had the energy of someone from the hood; her conversation sounded like someone who was well educated. The staff member and I immediately sparked a conversation because I must have stuck out like a sore thumb since most of the employees had severe mental illness.

The staff member introduced herself as Kim and we continued to converse about my life and my 'jobs' in my past. After the first conversation Kim and I had, she would coincidentally end up appearing every time I would take a break. During one of our conversations Kim gave me her number and told me to feel free to call her after work sometime. I began talking to Kim daily at work. After work, it wasn't long before Kim invited me to her house. I was no stranger to women; I knew what the invite was about.

I accepted Kim's invite and went to her house one night. As I expected it wasn't long before she seduced me. Kim informed me that her husband was incarcerated and she felt comfortable with me and wanted me to take some nude pictures of her to send to him. Of course, I agreed and I didn't make it past three pictures before we were having intercourse.

That night changed the dynamics of my work and home environment because a place that I was referred to that was supposed to help me only added extra stress to my mental state. Kim began to call me to her office throughout the day to talk on a personal level and would personally pick me up for work some days. Tee Tee began to become suspicious about the relationship that Kim and I had.

The sexual encounters with Kim and I started to happen on a regular basis and I could tell that she was becoming emotionally invested because she started to question the relationship I had with Tee Tee. She suggested that I end that relationship. Eventually the situation with Kim and I became so messy that I no longer had an interest in going to work there. Kim would always find a reason to call me to her office to discuss our personal relationship.

After a while I would no longer go to the mental health office for therapy or medication because I felt like it was a waste of my time. The medicine that I was being prescribed seem to enhance my mental health symptoms and the therapy was just pointless because it was a stranger that acted as though he knew and understood my problems from just seeing me once a week for 30 minutes to an hour which was illogical to me, even in my unstable mental state.

I continued to drink to self-medicate and also the petty drug dealing to make money which rarely was enough to cover rent or bills. Tee Tee began staying out at night and partying while leaving me home to watch her kids like I did for Diana in the past. To be honest, I used to be happy when she stayed out at night because I could relax and not deal with confrontational situations. At the time, I felt obligated to stay and help Tee Tee because of what she had done for me like signing my bond when she didn't really know me and letting me move in to her home when I was kicked out of Linel's house. But everyone has their limits and I reached mine.

One night Tee Tee and I had been drinking and an argument ensued and then the unthinkable happened. Tee Tee ran in the house and came back outside with a butcher knife. She began swinging it wildly at me and I jumped into it. At first, I did not realize that I was cut until I started feeling warm blood gushing down my leg. Tee Tee began to panic and cry but for some strange reason I felt sorry for her. The paramedics and police arrived at the scene and began to ask me questions about the incident.

I lied and told the authorities that I had gotten into a physical altercation with someone who tried to rob me. The police took the statement but appeared not to believe me. The thing I did to Keisha by breaking her jaw had now happened to me in a different way but with the same result by getting stabbed in the leg. Talk about karma. When I got to the hospital it was difficult for the doctors to stop the bleeding but thankfully they did. I ended up getting 28 staples in my leg, the same amount as when Keisha ended up getting her jaw wired. Karma is real!

Keisha was unable to eat for a month and when Karma came back around I was unable to walk for almost two months. When some of my family members found out about the incident, they were enraged and I could tell that a lot of them did not buy the story of me getting robbed by the expressions on their faces. My brother Pernell contacted me once he heard about the incident and insisted that I move back to DC because he feared for my life in North Carolina. I agreed to move back to DC but I didn't tell Tee Tee that I was leaving.

Once I healed enough to walk, I began making arrangements to move back to DC. The day I left North Carolina I told Tee Tee that I was going to the store but I knew I would never return from the store because not only was I not going to the store I had no intentions of ever coming back or contacting her ever again. I had never felt a true connection with her even though I grew to love her kids but even the love I had for her kids could not make me stay with her any longer.

The move back to DC lasted only five months. I reconnected with Frank and James but now they were no longer talking. Frank and I would hang out daily and

I reconnected with Diana and my daughters which was one of the only positive things that came out of my move back to DC. I had picked up another habit before my trip back home to DC and that habit was powder cocaine.

Pernell had no idea what he had gotten himself into by inviting me back into his home. A couple of months had passed and while I was high and drunk I decided to call Tee Tee to check on her and the kids. And to my surprise when she answered the phone she appeared to be overly excited as though a ghost had surfaced and began to cry and apologize about the stabbing incident. After the initial phone conversation, we began conversing daily and she always would insinuate that I needed to come back and that things would be different. I really didn't pay much attention to what she was saying because most of the time I was high and drunk.

One incident pushed Pernell to his boiling point. The incident that I am referring to is when Pernell had to go out of town on business and left me to oversee his household. At that time, my two younger nephews Donta and Torry who were 18 and 19 years of age, were visiting for the summer and my older cousin Walter who was also staying at Pernell's house. Pernell had just purchased a pit bull puppy before he left and gave me specific details on how to care for his dog.

106

On the night in question, Frank had come over to hang out with me and my nephews. Walter came into the house with a girl. The girl did not look hot, but cocaine and alcohol can make the best out of any situation. It just so happens that the girl that Walter brough home liked to drink and party and we had plenty to drink.

Before I knew it, the girl was in the room butt naked having sex with Walter and she signaled me to come and join and I did. Then before I knew it, my nephews and Frank were all participating in what is known as a 'train'. After we finished, the girl stated jokingly, "you guys are so nasty I rather suck the dogs dick" and just so happens, the puppy walked in front of her and she picked him up and proceeded to suck the puppy's dick.

When Pernell returned home he had no clue of the party that had taken place in his house just the night before and how his dog was molested by a strange woman. I later found out my cousin Walter was the 'snitch'. Pernell found out what had taken place in his absence and was furious and kicked everyone out of his house, even my two nephews that were visiting. I had only one other option and that was to take Tee Tee up on her offer to move back in with her.

By this time, Tee Tee had relocated to the capital of North Carolina, Raleigh, because she said it had more job opportunities. I had no problem with that since my older sister Beverly had just relocated to Raleigh, North Carolina with her new job. I traveled back to North Carolina but things were totally different this time because I did not know anyone in the town she moved to at all. The car I had was broken down and I was flat broke. Tee Tee didn't have a job but had gotten the house under the section 8 program so the rent was very low.

The peace between Tee Tee and I didn't last a week before we were back fussing and fighting. The financial situation had gotten so bad that I would steal toilet paper from the bathrooms of public places to take home. At one particular time the water had gotten turned off because we couldn't afford to pay the bill. It just so happened that the fire department was directly next door to the house Tee Tee and I were living in. I would make up bogus stories such as one of the water lines in the house busted and I needed to use their water until it was fixed so I would carry a big bucket to the fire department and fill it up with water daily for about two weeks and carry it back to the house so we could take baths, flush the toilets and eat.

By the time I scraped up enough money to get the water turned back on at home the gas got turned off.

Now mind you, two young kids were in the house at this time and the gas regulates the hot water and the heat in the house. We had to heat the house by turning on the electric stove and heating the water that way too in order to give the kids and ourselves baths.

Things were at an all-time low. The relationship between Tee Tee and I never grew, it just was something we both felt obligated to be in for some reason unknown. Tee Tee and I finally managed to get all the utilities turned back on and current because I started to find day laborer jobs. To add to Tee Tee and our dysfunctional relationship, she ended up getting pregnant. At that time I was dealing with no stable income, mental health issues and about to have a child with a woman that I did not feel emotionally connected to. The mental breakdowns began to increase and I could no longer control when they occurred. I could be in a conversation with someone and begin crying for no apparent reason.

Frank decided to come to North Carolina to visit me because we kept in contact. When Frank arrived, he looked at me in disbelief as though he had something to tell me but did not. Frank and I were hanging out one day during his visit and he said something that made me angry at the time but later made me aware. He told me 'man you fell off since you've been dealing with Tee Tee. As long as I've known you, I have never seen you living like this. This is not you.' I responded to him in a defensive way but inside I knew he was being truthful. Even though Tee Tee was pregnant, it didn't improve our communication because we continued to disagree about everything. We couldn't stand each other.

The holidays rolled around and I found a seasonal job at Honey Baked Ham. The job at Honey Baked Ham was about 3 ½ miles from where I was staying and I didn't have a car at the time. I had to start walking at least two hours before I was scheduled to work in order to arrive on time. The job at Honey Baked Ham helped me realize how insensitive people can be because one of the people that I worked with informed me that he lived no more than five minutes from me. He would drive past me sometimes on the way to work and sometimes I would be getting off work and he would not offer me a ride home.

We were going to the same place but I never complained or asked for his help because I knew how quick situations can change. I would laugh to myself when the people at the job would act as though they were better than me.

One night after walking home from the job, I had a breakdown and became overwhelmed with negative emotions. I was having thoughts of how I was failing as a father to my kids in DC and how I had practically turned into a bum and that my life was pointless. I had finally made it home and as usual Tee Tee and I started arguing about our financial situation. Tee Tee left the house.

I was enraged. I was stuck there with such bad thoughts, that I went to the cabinet and proceeded to continuously slit my wrists with the hopes of losing my life. By the time I cut enough, Tee Tee walked in, took the knife from me and the last thing I remembered was that I woke up in a mental institution. I stayed in the institution almost a month before I was released. While I was in the institution, my older sister Beverly would come see me and encouraged me to follow the rules of the institution.

North Carolina Department of Human Resources
Division of Mental Health, Developmental Disabilities
and Substance Abuse Services

Dorothea Dix Hospital
820 S. Boylan Ave.
Raleigh, NC 27803-2176

PRINT DATE / TIME Tue Jan 4, 2005 2:09 PM

PATIENT TYPE **INPATIENT**

CLIENT NAME/ADDRESS	WORK PHONE	MRUN #	EDUCATION LEVEL	SOCIAL SECURITY #
WINGATE, LINEL DION		1-04-62-45	TWELFTH GRADE	

	HOME PHONE	DATE OF BIRTH	AGE	RACE	NATIONALITY	SEX	MS	VET STATUS
RALEIGH, NC 27604		08/08/1975	29	B	NON-HISPANIC	M	S	NO

	MAIDEN NAME	PLACE OF BIRTH	LANGUAGE SPOKEN	RELIGION
		LEE	ENGLISH	BAPTIST

MOTHER'S MAIDEN NAME	FATHER'S NAME	ALIAS LIST
SOUTHERLAND	WILLIAMS, LINEL	

ADMIT DATE/TIME	ORIGINAL ADMIT DATE	ACCT #	COUNTY OF COMMITMENT	ADMT COMMIT TYPE	UPDATE ADMIT CURRENT TYPE	DATE CHANGED	ARRIVED BY
12/26/2004 10:00 PM	12/26/2004		WAKE	IMM			LAW ENFORCEMENT OFFICER

CURRENT LOCATION	COUNTY OF RESIDENCE	COUNTY OF RESPONSIBILITY	LIVING ARRANGEMENT AT ADMISSION	ACCOMPANIED BY
DISCHARGED	WAKE	WAKE	PRIVATE RESIDENCE	HAYLE, RALEIGH PD

CURRENT SERVICE/SERIES TYPE	EMPLOYMENT STATUS	ADMITTING DIAGNOSIS	ATTENDING PHYSICIAN
ADULT ACUTE PSYCH, ACTIVE	NOT EMPLOYED	REC DEPR PSYCH PSYCHOTIC	WEED, BARRY

MEDICAID #		REFERRAL SOURCE	COMMERCIAL INSURANCE NAME	ADMITTING PHYSICIAN
		WAKE AREA		MAYO, JAMES P
ANY ADVANCE DIRECTIVES? NO		REFERRAL AGENT	GROUP POLICY NUMBER	CONSULTING PHYSICIAN
		JENNY OWENS, MD		
		3000 FALSTAFF ROAD		OTHER
		RALEIGH NC 27619		
		919-250-3133		

PRIOR STATE FACILITY ADMIT	DATE DISCHARGED	PATIENT RELATIONSHIP
DOROTHEA DIX HOSPITAL	06/17/2004	MARY BRUTON-ABCDGHIJKMWYZ

LEGALLY RESPONSIBLE PERSON / NEXT OF KIN / CONTACT PERSON

	PRIORITY IV	PRIORITY V	PRIORITY VI
PRIORITY III			

RELATIONSHIP SISTER	RELATIONSHIP	RELATIONSHIP
PREF CONTACT METHOD	PREF CONTACT METHOD	PREF CONTACT METHOD
HOME PHONE	HOME PHONE	HOME PHONE
WORK PHONE EXT	WORK PHONE EXT	WORK PHONE EXT
CELL PHONE PAGER	CELL PHONE PAGER	CELL PHONE PAGER
FAX	FAX	FAX
EMAIL	EMAIL	EMAIL

COMPETENCY STATUS	DATE GUARDIAN QUALIFIED	LEGAL STATUS ON ADMIT	CONFIRMED?	UPDATED LEGAL STATUS	UPDATED
COMPETENT					

LEGAL CHARGE CATEGORY	SPECIFIC LEGAL CHARGES		ATTORNEY	
			PHONE	

DATE SCREENED FOR MR	SPECIAL CLIENT CATEGORY	OLMSTEAD	VISIT LOS	MED EXAM CASE	AUTOPSY	D/C REFERRAL
			2			3

DATE DISCHARGED	DISCHARGE/DEPARTURE REASON	D/C LIVING ARRANGEMENT	DISCHARGE DESTINATION ADDRESS	DOROTHEA DIX HOSPITAL	COUNTY WAKE
12/26/2004	TRANSFER TO MED/SURG BED INHOUSE	MSS		PHONE	

COMMENTS / REMARKS	DISCHARGE COMMENTS
NO INSURANCE ALL FORMS SIGNED /MS	

AUTHORIZING AREA PROGRAM	AUTHORIZATION #	AUTH FROM	AUTH THRU	NAME / PHONE # PERSON AUTHORIZING
WAKE AREA		12/26/2004	01/25/2005	GLORIA

Form No. DMH1-10-83 (rev.)

CERTIFICATION / FACESHEET

Upon my release the doctors suggested that I end my relationship with Tee Tee because it was unhealthy for my mental state but against the orders, I returned to the same situation that led up to my hospitalization. I began to diligently look for a job because I had another child on the way. I called every labor job listed in the phone book and asked if they were hiring and if the company didn't answer I would leave a message. I was so determined to change my living situation that I used what Frank told me as motivation to get back on top of my game financially and physically.

All my phone calls to different companies paid off because a moving company called me to set up an interview. I was in shock when the moving company contacted me because Tee Tee told me that I was lazy. She felt that because I would not apply to jobs in person that I could not get a job over the phone. My mantra had reappeared, 'Failure is not an option.'

When I went in for the interview the company hired me on the spot with very little work experience. I began to be focused on creating a comfortable living situation for the life that I was expecting in the world. I began working on my days off if the company needed any help. It didn't matter to me because I was never in a rush to get home. Even though I was still drinking alcohol I couldn't consume as much as I did in the past because I was working most of the time. The more I would work and gain financial security, the more I began to ignore the petty arguments with Tee Tee.

I reached a financial situation in which I started saving money. This was something I had never done when I was in the streets dealing with larger amounts of money. Tee Tee got herself a job at a nursing home and it just so happened to be a 3rd shift which worked out for me because when I would get home from work she would be asleep or getting ready to go in so it would just be me and the kids throughout the night. It made our unbreakable bond because I would help them with their homework, prepare them for school and sometimes let them stay up with me and watch TV. My bond with the kids didn't change the dynamics of my relationship with Tee Tee. To be honest I kind of liked things the way they were. There were no confrontations and few conversations between Tee Tee and I.

I realized that I had let my body and wardrobe go downhill so I decided to work on them both. My waist size was a 38-40 at the time and my goal was to reach a size 34. I made a deal with myself that when I reached a size 34 I would take myself shopping. I began going to the gym every morning before work to exercise and within two months, I reached my weight goal and that was definitely a confidence booster because women started flirting with me again.

Three months before Tee Tee was to give birth, we found out it was a girl. I know I needed transportation so I had saved enough money to put a down payment on a car. Linel and I had started speaking again and he let me know he was selling a car and that I didn't need a down payment. He would just take me to his bank to get a loan for the car he was selling which was a silver jaguar with a cream interior. The Jaguar was a beautiful car but Linel failed to tell me that the only reason he was selling the car was because he was having car problems. I would soon find that out after I purchased the vehicle from him.

A month before my daughter was born I had reconnected with my little brother and sister, Lee and Nefertiti. I felt like it was a better time for them to be reintroduced into my life because I was working a stable job, had gotten back into shape physically, and had just purchased a nice car from our father. Lee had a party going on the following week and thought it would be a good idea for me to come visit him at that time. The decision I made to go visit my little brother would change the course of my life.

Lee had graduated college in Virginia and moved to Charlotte, North Carolina which was two and a half hours from where I was currently living in Raleigh, North Carolina. When I arrived at my little brother's house, I admit I was a little impressed because he was in his early 20s and obviously made some good life decisions judging by the house in the neighborhood he was living in. When we greeted each other, and began talking I felt like we were never separated. It was an instant spiritual connection.

Lee and I discussed some of our past memories. One of our most memorable moments that we spent together was one Christmas that we spent with Linel. We observed there was a Christmas tree with a lot of presents underneath it. We both were excited and assumed that some of the presents had to be for us but to our surprise on Christmas morning the moment of truth, out of 10 to 15 presents that were under the tree maybe one belonged to Lee and I and the presents that we did receive were two unwrapped remote control cars and to top it off Linel didn't even put enough thought into it to get us some batteries.

As we laughed and talked about the past, Lee began to discuss his current situations with women that were going on in his life. I was a proud big brother at that point to hear my little brother's conquest of different women. Lee and I finally arrived at the party and a few of his friends including women they knew showed up. A strange thing happened while I was observing how Lee and his friends displayed a superior level of confidence that reminded me of a life that I once possessed.

That night I enjoyed myself. My spirit felt whole in a positive way. On the ride home, I couldn't stop thinking about how much I had really fallen off. I knew Frank was right when he told me I was going downhill in the relationship I was in, but that one night showed me that I wasn't being true to myself or my spirit.

When I returned home I had a totally different outlook on life and Lee and I began talking daily. I knew that the relationship I was in with Tee Tee wasn't for me and that I was just wasting her time and my time by continuing a relationship that wasn't meant to be. It wasn't that easy because I had a baby on the way with her. On July 2, 2006 Tee Tee gave birth to a beautiful baby girl with the fullest beautiful lips I had ever seen and we named her Niyanni JaKara. I enjoyed being a hands-on father for the first time, being that I was running the streets when my other two daughters Crystal and Lynette were born.

The more I began to be truthful with myself about how unhappy I was in my current living situation the more I realized I had to find happiness within myself so that I could give my newborn daughter a happy life. I had to make the difficult decision of leaving my baby to rebuild myself mentally and spiritually. I discussed with Lee my plans to relocate and he was cool with my decision being that he was a bachelor.

Now faith has it, the job that I was currently working at had a location in Charlotte, North Carolina not too far from where Lee lived. I informed my job that I would like to relocate to their Charlotte office and they made the proper arrangements. I gave my job a final date that I would be relocating myself in a position where I couldn't change my mind if I wanted to. Once I had all my arrangements in order I had a discussion with Tee Tee and informed her that I would be leaving and provided her with the specific date that I planned on moving out of the house.

Tee Tee must have believed that I was joking because she laughed in my face and told me with a smirk on her face "stop playing you know that you aren't going" in a sarcastic tone. I did my day-to-day routine up until the day that I was leaving. I told Tee Tee that I was about to go and she asked me when I would be back. I reminded her about the conversation we had a month prior to the date of me moving.

One of the first times I saw Tee Tee showing emotion was when I was loading my clothes into my car but strangely I had no feelings about her and could only think about Niyanni, my newborn daughter before I departed. I had a talk with the other two kids who had become a big part of my life and explained to them that I would no longer be around.

I held my newborn daughter for about 10 minutes while considering her eyes as she smiled and continuously told her that I loved her. I finally got in

118

my car and left but I did not have any feelings of remorse because deep inside I knew I had to remove myself from my current living situation for me to grow strong as a man. I felt extremely confident about my decision to move.

When I arrived at Lee's house in Charlotte he greeted me with open arms almost as though he had been waiting for this moment. The first couple of weeks were difficult for me to adjust to because Lee and I had never lived together. Once we realized each of our boundaries, we became inseparable. I began growing stronger spiritually by the day.

Diana and I started communicating on a regular basis and eventually Tee Tee would bring my daughter to visit me. As my confidence grew I began attracting a different class of people. When in the past all I would attract were people that were involved in illegal activities I now began to attract people that were creative, inspired, and self-motivated. As I continued to grow internally, I began having a different outlook on life. I was no longer content with working for someone because I started to feel like someone controlled my financial destiny. In the past even though I was involved in illegal activities I was still working independently and had more control over my financial stability.

I could no longer relate to my coworkers being happy accepting crimes for pay because I had already been exposed to a different lifestyle. I began being truthful with myself and realizing there is a big difference between a job and a career and couldn't understand how the owners of the company seem to always be happy or in a good mood while the employees would always be complaining and living in poverty. I considered that working to be poor. I understood that now I had myself as well as three kids to support so I continued to work the job but I never looked at it the same way again. I looked at it for what it was.

My relationship with Lee continued to grow more. We would converse and understand that we were the same but had been brought up in different environments. He would later expose me to how to budget and be responsible with money which I had never been in the past. Little did I know that my whole life was dying. I was being taken out of the situation with Tee Tee which happened to be one of the best conscious decisions I had ever made in my life.

I began dating different women but this time unlike the past, I was 100% truthful with them and that appeared to attract them more to me. About six months after leaving, Tee Tee and I decided to try to work on our relationship one more time. It seemed insane being

120

that I never had a connection with her. It felt like it was the right thing to do since I had a child with her. I decided to transfer my job once again and relocated back to Raleigh, North Carolina with Tee Tee. I had changed so much at that point that the relationship did not even last two months before I decided to leave for good this time.

My older sister Beverly also lived in Raleigh which also enabled me to stay with her until I could find a place. Her generosity surprised me due to how many times I had let her down in the past. I was still drinking at the time but the habit was limited because I had to work during the day. As I look back on the people and events that came into my life, I realized they were placed there for a reason and that led to me rebuilding and changing the course of my life in a positive way because situations and people could not be in my life this strategically by accident.

7   EVERYONE AND EVERY EVENT HAD A PURPOSE IN MY LIFE

I entered into a relationship that served a divine purpose in my life and directed me back to the path of my destiny. I appreciate the time people sacrificed to empower me. Empowerment has given me the tools to inspire and help change the lives of others who may be experiencing similar obstacles. I'm reminded of the symbolic bird, Phoenix. The phoenix, said to be reborn from ashes, provides the ultimate symbol of strength and renewal. It is a bird, with a long life, that achieves rebirth by going through a cycle. My spirit is akin to that of a phoenix, sent to be a messenger to others about the importance of preseverence.

I will not let the people who contributed to placing me back on course not be acknowledged and celebrated. The first person I met that would unknowingly assist me in my internal building stage was a young lady named Renée. I met Renée in the last place I expected to meet someone. I met her in a nightclub. Renée was a nice looking young lady who appeared to be well educated. I was instantly attracted to her by the way she pronounced her words and carried herself with class; plus she wasn't bad to look at. I spotted Renée sitting at a table with a couple of her friends moving her head as though the song that the DJ was playing was one of her favorites. I asked her to dance.

When I first asked her to dance she declined my offer stating that she just came to the club to hang out with her friends, not to meet people. I accepted the rejection from her and slowly walked away but as I walked away I could hear her friends encouraging her to take me up on my offer and while I continued to walk to the other side of the room I felt a tug on my arm and it was Renée, with a smile on her face, inquiring if my offer to dance still stood.

Renée and I danced all night and as we danced I would ask questions about her and volunteer information about myself over the loud music. By her body language I felt she was attracted to me because while we were dancing she would always push her body against mine as though she felt comfortable with me. Renée gave me all the signs that she had an interest in me but her actions showed differently. When she and her friends were leaving the club she just waved goodbye at me and as luck had it, I did not get her phone number at the club that night.

But I ran into her at a grocery store a couple of days later and to my surprise, Renée approached me and asked me if I remembered her from the club a couple of nights ago. Of course, I said yes and we continued to talk about how much fun we had conversing at the club so we exchanged numbers.

The same day we exchanged numbers she called me that night and we decided to see each other the following day. The next day we connected as planned and it was a great first date which would not be the last. The more I got to know her the more I grew attracted to her. As time went on we would talk two to three times a day for hours and I soon realized that Renée and I had similar backgrounds as far as family dysfunction and life experiences.

The relationship with Renée and I moved fast and within a month of knowing her she moved me into her place with her two kids but the difference between Tee Tee and Renée was that I had a connection with her. I would discuss with Renée my frustration with working a job and how I needed a career and she would always respond "what's holding you back pursuing a career versus the job?" My response was always "I need the money now and is just not a good time for me to leave my job." I decided to start seeking different employment opportunities but I, because I did not have

124

a college degree, was told I did not have the qualifications.

I felt stuck with no way out of the hell of living a life working for someone who was paying me crumbs. Renée and I discussed my need to further my education in order for me to work towards having a career. I had my back against the wall. I had to decide fast because I felt like the longer I worked for this job, the further I would fall behind in life which was true. I now had approached my late 20s.

I went to work one day not knowing it would be my last day. All day I had on my mind on how I was stuck if I did not further my education. I got ready to clock in and the supervisor told me that he wanted to meet with me later that day. I called Renée while she was at work and told her that I no longer wanted to have a job. I needed to go to school to further my education so I could build a career and she agreed and told me if I chose to leave the job that she made enough income to hold me down while I pursued school which was a green light for me to leave the job I was currently working.

The supervisor finally called me to his office for the meeting. The meeting consisted of him telling me how unsatisfactory of a job I had been doing lately for the company and at this point I had the green light to quit but I preferred him to fire me so I could receive unemployment benefits.

He sat back in his chair looking at me as though he controlled my life and threatened me by saying if you don't improve your work performance I must let you go. I looked at him and smiled and responded well why don't you let me go. He looked confused and powerless as though he did not understand my response. The supervisor then told me that he did not like my attitude. At that point I knew that he was going to do what I wanted him to do and that was fine by me.

I clocked in and in less than an hour after I clocked in I got a call to the office again but this time the whole resource department was at the conference table. I walked in relaxed and stared everyone in the face because I already knew what was about to take place. The supervisor explained to me that he had to let me go because of my poor performance on the job and sarcastically told me that he really did not want to fire me which I knew was a lie so I abruptly stopped him in mid sentence. I confirmed, "I'm fired right?" and he responded "yes." I then responded, "So I can leave now?" and he responded "no because I need you to sign a paper first."

I laughed at him and told him if I'm fired why would I have to sign a paper and he then told me

126

because we can give you a good reference for another job if you signed the papers. I looked the supervisor in his eyes as his pale white skin now turned red and told him how in the world could you give me a good reference if you fired me and that I wasn't signing any papers and I walked out and never looked back.

I informed Renée of what had just taken place and she laughed and insisted that I go down to the unemployment office to sign up for unemployment benefits. To my surprise, I found out that the papers that my supervisor wanted me to sign was a paper stating that I would resign from the job. Being that I did not sign the papers, it proved that they fired me so eventually I received my unemployment benefits.

I kept my word with Renée and enrolled in a GED class. My first day of class I felt a sense of freedom that I had never felt before and knew that I had made the right decision by choosing to further my education. Renée also kept her end of the bargain and held me down financially while I was attending school. The classes I took for my GED lasted a total of an hour and 30 minutes and that gave me plenty of time to drink. Even though I was doing something positive for myself my drinking habit had increased once again.

My relationship with Renée began to take a turn for the worst due to my drinking. I began being very obnoxious and disrespectful while under the influence of alcohol. What was first a fun and loving relationship had turned into some of my past dysfunctional relationships. Renée was extremely patient with my drinking and began to insist that I get some type of treatment but I would always decline the idea. Even with all the drinking I was doing at that time I somehow maintained a good grade average in school.

One night after heavily drinking while hanging out with Renée and her friends I had become extremely angry and an argument occurred between Renée and me. While in a drunken rage I pulled out a gun and put it to her head and threatened to kill her in front of her friends. Renée's friends began yelling for someone to please call the police and when I heard that I took the gun from her head and ran into the woods and stashed the gun. By the time I walked back up to the scene the police had arrived.

The police questioned me about the incident but I continuously told him that Renée and her friends were lying about me. The police must have believed what Renée and her friends told them because they locked me up and charged me with communicating threats and assault with a dangerous weapon without finding the gun. I was locked up under a high bond which no one was willing to pay.

I had to wait three months until a court date. On my court date, I walked in the courtroom and I saw

Renée sitting with the district attorney. The first thought that came to my mind was I was going to go to prison for a long time. Renée must have felt pity for me and informed the judge that she did not want to press charges; she just wanted me to get help with my drinking and wanted a restraining order placed against me.

The district attorney and my lawyer came to an agreement that I would have to participate in probation and the alcohol treatment program upon my release and that I could be released that day because my time was served. I was excited to be released from jail but heartbroken because I could no longer come within a certain amount of feet near Renée.

When I got released everything took a turn for the worse. I had lost everything; my car had gotten impounded and I no longer lived with Renée because of the restraining order. Unexpectedly, Renée had been saving my unemployment benefit payments while I was incarcerated and she contacted one of my friends and informed him that he could pick up my card.

The friend whom she called, I had met in my old neighborhood was from Virginia and moved to North Carolina with his wife and kids. His name was Rome. We had gained a brotherhood bond when we first met.

130

At the time we met we had a lot in common with relationship problems so we would hang out and drink and party and discuss how unhappy we were in our relationships.

Rome and I had a lot in common. He liked to drink and chase women just as I did and it wasn't long before I had considered him my best friend. When I was released from jail, I contacted Rome and he informed me that he and his wife were no longer together and that he had a bachelor pad and I was more than welcome to come stay with him. I accepted his offer and he really earned his stripes as a best friend because he would take me where I needed to go since my car was impounded.

He also worked as the liaison between Renée and I to settle our differences and collect money that she saved for me. About two weeks after living with Rome, he decided that he wanted to work things out with his wife and informed me that he would be leaving the state within a couple of weeks to reunite with his family. I was immediately in panic mode because I had to hurry up and find a place to live. My only best friend in North Carolina was about to move to another state. Thanks to Renée I could put down a deposit for a place if one was available and I had stable income from unemployment benefits to cover rent.

As faith had it, the first rental place I contacted had availability and informed me that I could move in immediately. Rome took me to look at the place. We both were impressed. It was a nice house in an upscale neighborhood. It couldn't have been at a better time because Rome would be leaving two days before I moved into the place.

When I moved into the place I had very little clothes, no TV or furniture, just myself. I was thankful to have a place to live and realized that all the material things were unimportant. I would find out that I had more going for me then just finding a place to live.

I had contacted the school that I was attending and explained to them my legal situation and they accepted me back in school to pursue my GED. The school that I was attending was 30 minutes away from where I had moved to and I no longer had a car. I could not let the opportunity to better my life be interrupted by lack of transportation so I learned how to commute by using public transportation.

The commute would take me two hours to get to class and two hours to get back if I was lucky and didn't miss the bus. I was determined to finish school by any means necessary. Rain, hail, sleet or snow I was at the bus stop waiting on the bus to transport me to school and never once complained about the four-hour trip to and from school for a one-hour class. I was still drinking but it was less often because I had the responsibility of paying rent.

I had no entertainment such as TV or radio so I began writing to my deceased mother during my free time at school and when I was home. I would update her about my life changes, the grandkids and expressing to her how much I missed and loved her. I built a relationship that I always wanted with her but was never able to obtain. So much so that I would feel guilty if I missed one or two days without speaking to her.

(8) I have a glem of hope that
i haven't felt in a long time
i know that it's only you. I wish
an hope i feel like this everyday
I pray for forgivness for all the
people that i have made feel bad
in the past an presnt in Jesus name
i wish you could be with me in
the disvssions i make. i know that
my father probl think that i have
let him down but thats not true.
I tring to do the wright thing
i wish you could touch him an
let him see that i am tring my best
I guess you can say i feel lonely no
i cant help to think about Teavsq an
esply yanni it not that i don't
about the other kids but it's just
shes so young an smart i really feel
like that about all the kids i just ha
an hard time showing emotion i don't
know why. i hope you can keep me
strong so 4 will not run Rose away
an let me give her time to think tee
now i see i am smothery her with
my love. i wish you could help me
give her a break an time to get things
together. I don't know why the bad
thoughts continvd to cross my mind
no trust mape because a lot of peopl
i put trust in seem to stab me in
the back. The only thing i know is that
you are on my side when people are against

134

...rew these trying times. I know you
...ember those well i finial got over her
...n havent spoken to her in 3mo so i guess

Dear Mom

I have been doing good i'm sorry
Mom i havent written you in a while. It's
kind of hard for me to focus because
i have a lot of stuff on my mind
i'm trying to deal with every thing
but its hard people say that i'm a
nice looking guy but it's hard for me
to believe because i don't believe it
some days are better than others to me
i now look in the mirrow an see
all the things i have done wrong
in the past to other people an realize i was wrong
at times i wonder why would i even
treat anyone the way i did i ask forgiveness
for all the wrong i have done to people
i would ask them to forgive me in their
heart because im truly sorry to any
i caused anyone i have hurt any
Mom i'm trying my best today even
studied at home i would just love
for the pain to leave Someone told me
that you have to have patience in
different situations, i don't know what
happen, i just feel bad. Could you
please bring me happiness
your son an Goodbye Dion with love

Dear Mom,
I haven't written you in a
while. I'm sorry 4 that but
you are always an still with
me. I would like to ask God
and you to please foregive me
for the wrong i have done
but i would in the same breath
say thake you for all the blessin
you are an have been giving to
me. I need to get back focus
so i can make my sprite an
my kidz proud. I hope you
enjoyed the visit we made
to you on motherday. it was
from the heart. Mom, i would like
the Higher Power an yourself to
bless me with a lot of money
so i can take ocare of myself
kidz an family all the time.

I can handle everyone problems but mine. I wonder do i miss ▮▮▮ because i lv her or because i ▮▮ her so wrong. I hope i can stay strong an maintain an wish that sh▮ ▮▮▮ follow her heart, if she really loves me an not family & friends. but i'll give it an break because to much calling an begg▮ will just run her away. Im try▮ to buid an relationship with all my kids to show them i care an miss them i feel alone a lot ▮ dont know what to do i gue▮▮▮ ▮▮ i feel alone i should study ▮o ▮▮ can get out of school. It ▮▮ ▮▮▮ ▮oint i don't know what to ▮▮▮ ▮ feel myself loseing faith ▮▮▮ I'd thankful for all y▮ ▮▮ i know the reason beh▮ ▮▮ not see them now bu▮ ▮▮▮ ▮▮e them soon. I hav▮ ▮▮▮ ▮eall now but i love ▮▮▮ ▮▮ you an know th▮▮ ▮▮▮ ▮▮ are with me you ▮▮▮ ▮▮y ▮▮ Then tell everyone ▮▮ ▮▮ ▮▮

137

Dear Mom

I have been lost latly. It's like i'm at a crossroad in my life, overall i want to do good but it seems the only way i can make people happy is to make money the wrong way. i just hope an pray that you will provid an way for me to make an great living so i can take care of myself and my kids an family. sometime i wish you were here with me to give me hope an guidance an support me in this. life struggle of good and bad. I guess things are harder 4 me because i really want to do what we call the right thing but it seems to confuss me because to me everyone who has wealth finicaly did some type of dirt. i feel bad that all the people i want to help stress me out if i can't. I just need you to show me another way so i can be myself and make a lot of money the right way, It's like my mind is fu an i just cant take anymore mento I need to feel great about myself.

Dear Mom

I know I have not written you in a while. Sm Since I was in collage or almost 3 years ago. I do have good news for you It's been three years since I had a drink and I see you loved answered my prayes by sending me a nice lady named ███████ Since I have been with ███████ I have started a bussiness and continu my education. I am very surprise at myself for almost making it threw a full semester with a full class schedual and with a great chance of passing On the down side I have been having a little financal problem it seems everything seems to be triy to block me from sucsess I ask that you and the family and frieds help remove the sprits that are and the people in which the sprites are working threw So I can reach the level of sucsuss that is already written for me. I have a record and clothing line. I have two artis that are extremly talented

For once in my life I truly did not feel alone. I knew my mother was with me. I would always end our conversations by jokingly telling her to tell my great grandmother Edith and my grandmother Annie Mae and my Uncle Deberry to behave and that I loved them. After the first month in my place I had the bus schedule down to a science. I began to take pride in my determination to make it to class by any means necessary and no one controlled my destiny but me.

Renée faded away on my path but I do understand that without her I would not have started my internal growth which enabled me to continue my education. With classes during the week and homework on the weekends I had no personal life. The only relationship I had was with my mother and at that time that was enough for me because she filled the void in my life and never judged me on any mistakes I made throughout life. I became completely honest with her in my writings. I confided in her how I mistreated people and hadn't been the best father to her grandkids and I would sometimes ask her what I could do to change the wrong that I had done to so many people. She would always respond in silence which I interpreted as her saying, 'only I could change myself.'

Throughout my transition in life the second person that would unknowingly assist me in my internal growth would be a young lady named Linda.

Linda played one of the most important parts in the second phase of my life. Linda was an extremely intelligent, attractive older lady with the most beautiful long legs I had ever seen.

I met Linda at a cookout at the home of a mutual friend of ours. When I first met Linda, she had no interest in me or so I thought, because she declined my advances. I felt like I had lost my touch since I had not approached any woman that sparked my interest since Renée and that had been almost a year prior. I did not give up and was very persistent trying to get to know this lady who looked as though she did not belong in the environment we were in. She wore high heels and dressed very conservative while most of the women at the cookout were dressed in urban wear.

Linda must have gotten tired of my advances and began to converse with me but her body language showed little interest in the small talk. After conversing for 10 to 15 minutes I asked for her phone number. I should've known that something was wrong because she gave me her phone number without hesitation.

The next day I decided to give Linda a call only to find out she had given me a wrong number. I was outraged and that was a big blow to my ego so I called our mutual friend and expressed my anger because of her giving me the wrong number.

Our mutual friend laughed and told me to hold on but little did I know he was calling Linda on a conference call so she could defend herself. When our mutual friend told me "you tell her what you told me' I got completely quiet. I got the courage to inform her about the discontent I had with her giving me the wrong number and she responded to me that I appeared to be arrogant and a womanizer because of my approach. She further stated that she had seen my type before and had no time for games.

After going back and forth on the phone our mutual friend must have found our insults amusing because I could hear him laughing in the background. Toward the end of the conversation, we began discussing things we had in common and Linda finally gave me her correct phone number.

Linda and I began conversing on a regular basis and occasionally having lunch together. Unlike the women in my past, my relationship with Linda blossomed into an awesome friendship without the complications of a committed relationship.

I began feeling comfortable with myself around Linda and would ask her advice about personal

142

situations I was dealing with such as my two daughters in DC and my strained relationship with my youngest daughter's mother Tee Tee. She would always encourage me to continue to reach out to the mothers of my children so I could at least build a cordial relationship for my kids' sake.

As time went on a bond grew between us and we would help each other. She would help me with difficult homework assignments and some days even take me to school. One day I came home from a long day of school only to find a note on my room door and the landlord stating that he was going to raise the rent an extra $40 per month.

I was furious about the unexpected rate increase because I was barely making it with the unemployment benefits I was receiving when calculating my food and travel expenses to and from school. I contacted Linda, which by then she had become my best friend and told her about the rent increase.

Linda suggested that I leave the house that I was currently living in and pay her half the rent I was paying there to save money so I could find another place to live. I took Linda up on her offer because I trusted her judgment and it sounded like a good plan. Unlike in the past when I would avoid difficult situations by just leaving, I faced the situation with the landlord in a professional manner and informed the landlord that I could no longer afford to live in that rental property due to the rent increase and asked if he could give me 30 days to evacuate the premises. The landlord agreed to give me 30 days and I agreed to let them keep the deposit as a last month rent.

The transition moving in with Linda was easy since we had already developed such a close friendship. Linda gave me a support system that words could not explain even though I was still drinking but I was more focused than I had ever been. I finally could see the hope and promise for my life.

The first four months of Linda and I living together was like first hand training on how to be a gentleman. Linda would help me to expand my vocabulary by using words that I was unfamiliar with during our daily discussions and explained to me the proper context in which to use the words as well as the meanings.

I began to develop a need to better myself and Linda was the liaison between my old world to the new one because of her exposure to the high society of life. With the assistance and support of Linda, I finished school and obtained my GED and that was a liberating feeling. It was the first time in my life that I had committed to a positive task and completed the task. At that very moment I realized that anything was possible if I stayed focused.

As soon as I obtained my GED my next step was to enroll in college so I enrolled in the local community college for social work but classes did not start until four months after I had enrolled. That meant I had free time and in the past free time meant trouble for me. But fortunately I spent my first couple of weeks preparing for an upcoming placement test.

Time would eventually not work in my favor because my drinking habit began to reach its peak once again and by the third week until starting college I was out of control once again. A neighbor must have called the police because of the loud disturbances that I was causing which lead up to me getting locked up for assaulting my best friend during a heated argument over my out of control drinking habit.

Linda had confronted me about not financially taking care of the agreement we made upon moving in with her because I began spending most of my money on alcohol and the alcohol took total control of the situation. On my ride to jail I had no clue of the severity of what had just taken place. In my mind I thought I would be getting out the next day. Things didn't work out as I thought due to my past criminal record. My bond was set really high.

That day I was sober and dressed in an orange jumpsuit. I felt the disappointment, but this time not about what I did to someone else but what I just had done to myself. Out of all the times I had gotten locked up in the past, this was the only time that I had a plan and goals to accomplish and had less than two months before I was to start my first semester of college. I came to the realization that I had jeopardized everything I had worked for in the last two years within a split second.

I was no longer in denial; alcohol played a part in every bad decision and broken relationship I had. I started back writing to my mother and asked her to please forgive me for my unacceptable behavior in the past and present. In fact, I needed her more than ever. I asked her to please help me find a way to stop drinking alcohol.

My mother must have heard me because the very next day after asking for help I had a spiritual moment. That morning I followed my daily routine by coming out to eat breakfast and returning back to my cell but this morning was different. When I closed my eyes to sleep, tears began rolling down my face as a type of imagery began to flash throughout my mind of the faces of all the people I had hurt.

It felt like my eyelids were glued shut because I could not open them. It was almost like I was forced to watch the chaos I had caused in other people's lives and as the people's faces flashed in front of me that I hurt, somehow I would feel the exact emotion they felt at that time. I honestly have no clue how long this experience had taken place but I do know when I finally opened my eyes, I did not feel like the same person.

I began writing apology letters to the people I had hurt recently and, in the past, even though I had no way of locating or contacting them. I felt like a new person and when I looked out of my cell window on this cloudy day, the clouds parted and the sun came out. I interpreted the sun breaking through the clouds as giving me a final chance to stay on the course that was chosen for me.

That day I know it was some sort of a spiritual cleansing because I no longer carried the burden of my past. I remained in my cell for the remainder of that day crying and giving thanks to the Most High for having mercy on my soul. I promised that when I would be released I would change my ways and no longer drink alcohol.

My second chance at living a productive life was granted. The Most High really did have mercy on my soul because out of nowhere my court date was moved back a month early and I was released from jail two weeks before the college semester would start. Linda had found it in her heart to forgive me for my disruptive behavior and welcomed me back into her home.

Within the first hour of my release, I kept the promise I had made with the Most High and enrolled in an alcohol treatment program. The program that was recommended to me was a paid treatment program and at that time I had little to no money to commit to paying for treatment but as fate would have it, until this day I still can't explain how I got in the program for free.

I had an agenda and I stuck to it. I accepted responsibility for my actions and I did something I never had done before. I contacted Diana and told her how good of a job she was doing raising my girls and that I apologized for the things that I had done to her in the past. I told her I would like to start being a father to my girls.

Diana appeared to be at a loss for words because all I heard was appreciation in her voice from the acknowledgment of her sacrifice for my girls and for me as though that was all she wanted to hear from me for years. Diana apparently felt the sincerity in my voice because ever since that day we built a strong friendship and began co-parenting our two daughters. I also contacted Tee Tee and worked out our differences and became an active father in my daughter's life as well.

My first week out of jail I connected with the mother of my kids to become active in their lives and was actively in an alcohol treatment program. The alcohol treatment program was late in the evening and lasted 2 ½ to 3 hours, three days a week. I never missed a day of class. I was always there at least 10 minutes ahead of time.

Linda continued to support and encourage me in gaining my sobriety. She took me to class and reviewed recovery material with me. I admit that some days were easier than others during my recovery process. As I grew further in my sobriety I began to realize a lot of my broken relationships with family members slowly began to heal. The interests I had in the past no longer entertained me, such as the multiple women.

I began finding comfort in educating myself about mental health and alcoholism so in the future I could help other people transition into sobriety without going through all the hell I went through and put people through.

The first semester of school had begun and I was extremely focused. It just so happened that all my classes had been set for early morning classes and did not interfere with my alcohol treatment classes. I felt purpose in life going to college and being sober - two things I could never imagine myself doing. Just because I was doing things that were positive in my life did not eliminate obstacles. The only source of income that I was receiving at the time was unemployment benefits and that had begun to flash throughout my mind. My financial responsibility still was a reality.

For the first month I got little help from family and friends which I expected to support my movement in the positive direction I was working on. But one person who did was my little brother. Lee resurfaced and being that he was doing pretty well for himself he began helping me with the bills and acknowledged his admiration for the progress he saw me making in my life.

Lee and I began talking every day about different subjects. No longer did we talk about women and partying. We would discuss goals and what possible job opportunities that I could explore. I was very thankful for my little brother assisting me in my time of need but after a while I couldn't accept another man, even though he was my brother, taking care of me.

I began to diligently look for employment between the time at school and the treatment program I was enrolled in. I had very little luck with finding employment due to my past record. I received a call from Lee one day with excitement in his voice telling me that he met a guy that owned a moving company in the town I was living in and that he was hiring. I was overwhelmed with joy and followed through with all the information Lee gave me.

I was hired and began working for the moving company. I would arrive at work ahead of schedule and stay as long as they needed me, which was mostly on the weekends because I did not have classes for treatment or college. The job was going great. I was busy and had no free time but I felt like a man because I was earning my own money while at the same time investing in my future.

Another obstacle would soon appear. I was called to the office of the supervisor and he informed me that he had to let me go because of my past criminal record. I was disappointed in the system in our society because in my mind I was doing everything that society encourages people to do to be successful but the rules did not apply to me. With my world closing in, I went back to the only hustle I was good at but this time would be different because I had a sober mind.

I connected back with my old contact in North Carolina and started conducting business as usual but this time I had a plan and my plan was not to work. No one was going to be in control of my own destiny. This time while conducting business, I was saving money and investing it into my own equipment and resources for the scam so I could work for myself.

151

Once I began working for myself a whole other world opened up to me. I could now take care of myself and my responsibilities such as my kids. I made a promise to myself that I would only do this until I could find a legitimate way to make income. I was a lot more responsible with my money than in the past because I paid off my probation fees and began to pay back Lee the money that he had given me in the past.

The scam that I worked for all those years making others money I was now running the show with no overhead. Unlike the past, I paid the people that were jeopardizing their freedom to feed their families or to keep a roof over their head a higher percentage than any of my old business partners could imagine because now I sincerely cared about people and their wellbeing and not just money and understood how unfair society could be because of what I had just experienced from the job situation. The business I was involved in did not affect my performance in school or my sobriety.

My relationship with Linda began to dissolve the more I grew financially and in my sobriety. I had no clue that the whole-time Linda and I were friends she was hiding that she was sick. I knew she had diabetes but no clue she had cancer. Linda began getting sick and going back and forth to the hospital and honestly, I felt like all the running around helping me get my life on track would be a burden to her health improving. I informed Linda that I would be moving out of her house within a couple of months but I would continue to help her anyway I could.

I felt torn because I had to make the decision to leave the home of the only person at one point in time that believed in me and encouraged me to better myself and helped to rebuild my self-confidence. Ultimately, I felt it would be the best decision for her and that way she could focus on getting better. In the process of finding a place I met the third person that would unknowingly assist me in my internal growth during my process of transitioning from Linda's home.

I ran into a young lady named Cynthia who I had a brief physical relationship with in the past. We always kept in contact and kept each other informed on the current situations that were going on in our lives. During our conversation, Cynthia discussed a rocky breakup from a long-time boyfriend and how she was recovering from a recent accident and we exchanged numbers once again.

Being that we were both in emotionally difficult situations we began talking daily about our current situations. Things began moving faster than previous relationships but this time things were different because I had no motive and was well aware of what I wanted in a relationship without the clouded judgment of alcohol.

I began spending most of my free time between classes and my side business with Cynthia.

While at home Linda and I were on good terms she had accepted the fact that I would be moving out soon and understood that I would still help her anyway I could. I knew deep in my heart that I wouldn't be in the position that I was in at that point in time if it wasn't for her and I verbally gave Linda credit and often acknowledged to her that she played one of the most, if not the most, important parts of my growth as a man.

Eventually Cynthia and I began a serious relationship and the fact that I was living with another woman regardless if she was my best friend did not sit well with Cynthia. One day Cynthia gave me an ultimatum, 'either you move in with me until you find a place or I can no longer deal with you if you continue to live with Linda.' By this time, I was completely in love with Cynthia and I loved Linda but in a different way. I knew I had to make the decision sooner than I anticipated. I explained the situation to Linda and she said she understood but her eyes said something different. I knew she had grown attached to me because she practically rebuilt me.

I finally moved in with Cynthia and things were going like I envisioned my ideal relationship would be. Cynthia and I would always be out doing something

154

together. Cynthia had two kids who I gravitated towards fast and they did likewise to me. The oldest of the two kids, Laura, was disabled and couldn't walk and had a speech impairment but we grew a special bond. Cynthia and her kids became my extended family because now I had regular contact with all three of my kids and the youngest who lived in North Carolina I would pick up every weekend and keep her sometimes during the week.

I had never imagined that life could feel so good. That I would be making money with my business, be in a relationship with the woman I loved and have a strong relationship with my kids. I began to feel that my life had value now and began looking for ways to exit out of the illegal business so I explained to Cynthia my concerns about my freedom and she suggested that I start my own business which sounded good but I had no idea of what business I wanted to get involved in.

One day while I was downtown, I ran into a young lady who recognized me from a club I used to go to years prior. The young lady spoke with me and she informed me that she was a rapper that was looking for management and asked me if I knew anybody that would be interested in managing her. I told the young lady who introduced herself as Lisa a.k.a. Flow that I would contact her if I ran across someone who could possibly help her.

155

We exchanged numbers and out of the blue one night I received a text from Flow stating that she would be performing at a bar downtown and it would be cool if I could come out to support her. The day of the show I was home alone because Cynthia had gone out with her friends. I decided to go check out the show where Flow was set to perform since I had nothing else to do. I walked in the bar and ordered a cranberry juice because I no longer drank alcohol and waited patiently for the show to begin.

Flow must have spotted me through the crowd because she ran up and greeted me like she was advised when I would show up. Finally, it was Flow's time to perform and she was really good with the exception that I thought her music could use some improvements. As I watched her perform, I thought with some help and a little guidance, Flow could be a successful artist.

When I got home I explained to Cynthia with excitement that I wanted to start a record label and I already had a possible artist in mind. I explained to Cynthia who looked confused as I was explaining the passion and stage presence of the artist that I had in mind and how with a little work she could be successful. Cynthia was apprehensive but suggested that I do a little research on the industry and the artist that I planned on signing to my label.

I started doing my research immediately. I had Flow send me every link she had on YouTube and listened to every track on the CD she gave me. I was determined; I knew this was the path that I was supposed to be on with no question because it felt natural. After doing all my research on Flow, I realized that she was a talented young lady. After talking it over with Cynthia, I called Flow and asked her if she would like to be the first artist on a record label I was starting.

She said yes and I began the process. I had a record label but without a name for the label. I subsequently named it the first name that constantly came to my mind which was "Failure Not an Option" because the name embodied everything that built me into the man I had become. For short I would call it F.N.O.

I had a name for the label and now I needed a logo. I had an original tattoo on my chest that symbolized perseverance so I used that as my logo. I couldn't have a record label without a music producer so I contacted one of my cousins, John who I hadn't talked to in over

10 years. He produced music for a local record label years prior. I asked if he would provide me with some tracks and give me some insight on the industry since he had experience in it. Without question he came on board.

I knew that I would need a studio to record in so I contacted another guy named Joe who used to record tracks for a rap group that I was a part of that consisted of one more member Leroy back when I was a kid and fortunately he had a studio but his son was running it and that was good for me.

Everything was falling into place. I let Cynthia handle the paperwork, such as emails and contracts, while I was the visionary; so, I handled the artist's image concepts of the song and executively produced every song. I finally found a legal job one that felt natural and I loved doing it.

Flow and I would constantly be on the phone discussing ways to improve her image and different marketing strategies that could get her noticed once we began recording. After weeks of going through different producers' beats there was finally one that stood out to me. It had heavy drums and a slow melodic reggae feel to it.

The first time Flow heard the track, she began writing immediately and two days later we were in the studio recording our first song together. The first day in the studio was magic. The chemistry between Flow and I was undeniable. I would catch the smallest details such as word pronunciation and would make sure that Flow's rhyme pattern matched the music. After the studio session, I had the files we recorded sent to John so he could master and edit the song.

The wait was torture, I had no idea what to expect. All I heard of my product was what was played back in the studio and that was far from a finished product. Two weeks had passed and I received a call I had been waiting for from John. He told me to check my email and sent me the final copy of the track he mastered. I was so nervous and excited I didn't remember telling him goodbye, I just hung up the phone and went directly to my email.

I paced around the room for at least 10 minutes before I opened the file. I had a lot riding on this project being a success because I invested everything I had passionately and financially. When I plugged in my headphones, I opened the file and I was overjoyed after hearing the final product.

I now knew to trust my instincts. I cried tears of joy that day because I manifested the thought into reality and I knew that limitations did not exist for me at that point. At that moment, everything that I had been taught about what I needed to obtain and do to be considered successful, i.e. material items or a title, did not mean success. However, when I envisioned something and made it into a reality, that was being successful.

Once I realized I was already successful, the world wasn't big enough for my creativity. A couple of weeks after I got the track from John, I had envisioned a video for the song with motorcycles and crowds of people in the party scene. I told a couple of people about my idea and they laughed and told me it would be impossible for me to do. But with me understanding that I manifest what I envision, I would laugh at them with their doubt in me.

The truth is I did not know anyone in a motorcycle club nor did I deal with a lot of people but I knew that I could manifest what I envisioned into reality. To no surprise, my very first video with Flow turned out to be more over the top than I envisioned. The video was filled with lots of people and lots of custom motorcycles decorated with chrome and neon lights.

Everything was moving at a steady pace with my company where I was employing a lot of people in the community but had very little money coming back in. I had to find a way to generate income from what I enjoyed doing. I received an email one day from someone who had seen Flow's video and inquired

160

about the shirts everyone had on in a couple of the scenes.

The gentleman went on to tell me that he had just opened a store at the mall and wanted to purchase some of my shirts to sell at his store. The shirts the guy was referring to were shirts I had made with my company's logo just for that specific video; but, I did not tell that to the guy that was inquiring about the shirts. I just took his order as though I had been selling T-shirts.

The gentleman that ordered the shirts for his store unknowingly opened the new entity for my company, merchandising. The more I began to grow internally the more Cynthia and I began to drift apart. The relationship that was once filled with discussions about a future together turned into discussions about bills and tasks. Cynthia and I became like strangers.

She wanted me to pay more attention to her emotional needs while I devoted all my time and energy to my creative needs which would end up being the demise of our relationship and the growth of my company.

To be truthful, I felt as though Cynthia deserved to be happy but I wasn't the man that could provide that for her because I wasn't letting anybody or anything stop me on my path. Eventually, Cynthia and I parted ways but not on a bad note. We both concluded that things just weren't working out between us.

I continued pushing forward with my record label and signed a couple of more artists. A cousin of mine named Dana who was already in fashion suggested that I begin marketing my T-shirts in fashion shows. I took her suggestions and to my surprise actual designers began to request my T-shirts to be featured in their fashion shows. My communication with Linda became nonexistent due to her getting into a serious relationship. I was a little disappointed not being able to share my progress with her since she played a major part in my transition into a man but I understood.

Additionally, I developed a need to help people so I became active in the community hosting free events

162

with different community organizations that served the less fortunate and organized free networking events for small business owners to promote their businesses.

Once I finished my second semester of college I didn't return but as fate had it, I got the opportunity later to work in the mental health field.

Once I began accepting responsibility for my actions and realized I had the power to control the path and direction that I wanted my life, I developed a personalized plan for myself which made me aware of the damage that I was doing to myself internally and physically.

On a daily basis, I began meditating, exercising and reading any literature that I felt could help me understand the power of the energy we all have within. In doing so, I was able to build my spiritual and physical awareness which gave me the strength to become absent of the demons such as alcohol and other unhealthy addictions that tortured my soul.

The self-awareness discovery I made assisted me with overcoming the diagnosis of depression and bipolar diagnosis that I was once given by mental health specialists. I realized this discovery process could also benefit the mental health community, as well as the substance abuse programs and agencies. I was in a better position to assist with their understanding that sometimes it takes more than the clinical aspect of mental health and addiction specialists to rebuild what some call a broken spirit.

From my observations of mental health, I now know that it takes someone who has mended their broken, lost spirit to rebuild a more powerful spirit that helps guide the people (in addition to the mental health specialists) that are trapped in the dark. Someone who can help them find their way through their mental health /addiction into the light of recovery, freedom and independence. I understood that the majority of the research done in mental health was based on test studies. To my knowledge, there had not been any prior test case that had overcome the diagnosis I was given without extensive medication and therapy.

I am a living breathing success case study. I am living a productive, functional life, without the lifelong medication or the prescribed therapy.

I have maintained my sobriety for over five years and had the discipline to stop smoking cigarettes, one of the most addictive legal drugs. I was smoking two packs of cigarettes a day and was drinking some sort of alcohol beverage from when I got out of bed until I went to bed.

The Higher Power energy can travel through anyone because as I look back, the last three people I discussed were strategically placed in my path for different stages of my growth.

Renée was placed in my path at the beginning of the building stage of my internal growth to give me the opportunity to further my education which would serve as the foundation of my journey.

The second stage which I consider one of the most important, was when Linda was placed in my path at the maintenance stage of my internal growth. This stage enabled me to build my self-confidence and awareness and to give me the opportunity to complete what I started in the first level.

The third person, Cynthia, was put on my path for the rebirth stage of my internal growth. As a spiritual person, I had the opportunity to let the first and second stages cultivate my purpose within. Throughout all the ups and downs I had experienced, nothing changed in my life until I changed my mind set.

As I continued on my path I began to genuinely want to help people that were in difficult situations such as alcoholism and mental illness. I know first-hand the internal hell they must be dealing with trying to understand why the cycle they appear to be caught in keeps repeating itself. I began to reach out to different agencies that dealt with troubled youth, adults and even the local school systems to volunteer. However, the only response I got was, 'I will call you.' To my dismay, the calls never came.

I had come to the conclusion that no one really wanted to help the youth or troubled adults. With every rejection I grew stronger and knew that I could do whatever I set my mind to do because of all the entities that I brought into reality from just a thought.

I stayed on my path and one day while sitting home I received a phone call. On the other end of the phone was my sister Beverly and she informed me that she had met a young man that worked for a mental health agency that would provide me with a paid opportunity to help people with a similar background as me. Beverly gave me the information to call the young man and everything she told me was true. The young man and I conversed about an hour and he explained to me the steps that I needed to take in order to become a certified peer support specialist.

I followed through with all the information the young man gave me and went to all the training and completed the course. The first couple of months working as a peer support specialist I began to notice a pattern in the consumers. It seems as though when they first would start the services they would be excited and motivated about a new beginning but after a couple months of seeing different doctors their whole mood and motivation dropped to an all-time low. I could relate to what they were going through because I knew the stress of seeing all these different doctors that were telling them all the same stories that made them feel miserable and depressed in the first place. No one had any answers and if they did it was never anything that they could relate to or could benefit them because there was, and still is, a cultural divide between the doctors and the clients. The doctors could not understand a lot of the situations that were causing the clients to be depressed.

I constantly observed all of my consumers' behavior but never voiced to them my opinion at the time but later these would become facts. I began sitting in counseling sessions with my clients with their consent and would observe their body language and the counselor or psychologist and see their disconnect. I would watch as psychiatrists would prescribe these once semi functional people with different dosages of medication as if they were lab rats to see what would work.

After working in that field for a couple of months I began to realize by working on the opposite side that a lot of the so-called professionals had no compassion for consumers in difficult situations because they could not relate and I knew this for a fact because I too had experienced the same disconnect with a lot of mental health professionals.

I started conversing with the owners of different mental health agencies and giving them pointers on how their company could possibly be more effective for the consumers because of my firsthand knowledge. As the demand for my inquiries grew, I had to start setting up meetings and once I began setting up meetings I began charging for my consultations.

I knew the routine because I once was a lab rat for the mental health industry that almost took my life. Another troubling factor in the mental health system I began to question was the need for a counselor, psychologist, psychiatrist, and the family specialist. I now understand that without a doubt in my mind it's all about money, insurance or that Medicaid pays all these different entities for practically no positive results for the clients. If any of these services were effective there wouldn't be the need for so much medication and people would not need the services for most of their life. I view a success story as someone who received these services and went on to live independently not dependent on the medication and these services for life.

I understand that it is impossible to truly know someone by seeing them once or twice a week for an hour at a time when there are people that have known them all of their lives and never knew they were dealing with certain issues. You would think someone could be more open with a complete stranger that he cannot identify with culturally or socially. The more I started to pay attention to the news and different events, I noticed that a lot of the people that were doing heinous crimes were under some type of psychiatric care and that's factual.

Living in my truth and the destiny bestowed upon me, began the moment I stopped seeing all the "professionals" who had no clue of what a day in my shoes was truly like; I also stopped all the different medications that were being given to me. I realized I was a test subject. A lab rat. I slowly became functional and productive in society. By no means am I discrediting anyone's profession. However, I am providing the reader an honest account based on my experiences with the mental health system and the people that I have worked with who are currently in the system. I have become conscious of the fact that human behavior cannot be predicted because environments and situations change constantly. However, I recognize that people respond differently to a person that they truly feel understands them. They appear to be inspired by people that have overcome similar circumstances.

I began setting up meetings with different agencies and discussing with them ways that they could improve relations with their employees and consumers. Before I knew it, different agencies were contacting me for my input and I realized that my past experiences had value. I started Dion Wingate Consultancy as a way to advocate for the unheard voices of people trapped in the mental health system as I had been.

Through this agency, I began building relationships with government officials, law enforcement personnel, and community leaders to assist the agencies/programs with understanding the issues that plague poverty stricken communities. I give back to the communities that I once destroyed by independently sponsoring mental health awareness events, local business networking mixers and clothing drives for the people that are facing financial hardship.

DION WINGATE CONSULTANCY, INC.

I now know my purpose while on earth is to motivate and inspire people who have lost faith in humanity. I want those who have lost faith to become aware that there are people of the human species that have compassion.

I created Dion Wingate Consultancy to advocate for the consumers who don't understand their rights. I help each person create a customized plan that includes the programs and agencies that will be most beneficial in improving the lives of those who suffer with mental disease and/or substance abuse addictions. The customized plans also include activities that will enable them to become self-aware functional, and productive citizens.

I spent over half of my life searching and looking for validation from others when the only validation I needed was the person I saw in the mirror every day. I understand that the Higher Power gives everyone different paths in life so everyone has a special story and mine is no more important than anyone else's. I shared some of my real life experiences to make someone else's journey easier and to remind them that it is okay to let people and things go throughout one's life. Maybe you are only meant to be at a level of internal growth for that person or vice versa just for that specific time in both your lives.

I rebuilt myself with the help and guidance of people on my path, and made the ultimate decision to stay on my life's course.

There are experiences that we may share with one another. However, everyone's path is different. Don't allow yourself to be so focused on the destination, that you forget to experience the journey. While on your journey and despite any obstacles, remember: Failure's Not An Option.

EPILOGUE

It was a long time ago,
I have almost forgotten my dream.
But it was there then,
In front of me,
Bright like sun-
My dream.

And then the wall rose,
Rose slowly,
Slowly,
Between me and my dream.
Rose slowly, slowly,
Dimming,
Hiding,
The light out my dream.
Rose until it touched the sky-
The wall.

Shadow.
I am black.

I lie down in the shadow.
No longer the light of my dream before me,
Above me.

Only the thick wall.
Only the shadow...

My hands!
My dark hands!
Break through the wall!
Find my dream!
Help me to shatter this darkness,
To smash this night,

To break this shadow
Into a thousand lights of sun,
Into a thousand whirling dreams
Of sun!

As I Grew Older
~ Langston Hughes

"The world is our classroom and life is our teacher."
~Dion Wingate~

ABOUT THE AUTHOR

Dion Wingate was born in Sanford, North Carolina, and raised in Washington, D.C. He started F.N.O. Clothing in 2012. Currently, Dion is the founder and executive director of Failure is Not an Option Organization. This organization mentors at- risk youth, ages 13-19.

Dion engages with those in the community who share similar interests of serving and advocating for those in need. Those needs include mental health awareness, allocating for resources, and education. The mission of the organization is to inspire others that have experienced obstacles on their journey. Ultimately, Dion endeavors to guide those on their own journey in the circle of life.

Made in the USA
Middletown, DE
23 September 2020